I0804854

Ball State Men's Basketball

1918–2003

The 1932-33 Ball State yearbook photography editor gets fancy, superimposing three Cardinal players on a campus scene.

Ball State's outstanding "Motown trio" from the late 1980s and early 1990s. Standing are Curtis Kidd (left) and Paris McCurdy. Scott Nichols is kneeling. The basketball rich Detroit area was one of the first places outside Indiana where the Cardinals had significant recruiting success.

BALL STATE MEN'S BASKETBALL
1918–2003

C. Warren Vander Hill and
Anthony O. Edmonds

ARCADIA
PUBLISHING

Copyright © 2003 by C Warren Vander Hill and Anthony O. Edmonds.
ISBN 978-0-7385-3163-2

Published by Arcadia Publishing
Charleston, South Carolina

Printed in the United States of America

Library of Congress Catalog Card Number: Applied for.

For all general information contact Arcadia Publishing at:
Telephone 843-853-2070
Fax 843-853-0044
E-mail sales@arcadiapublishing.com
For customer service and orders:
Toll-Free 1-888-313-2665

Visit us on the Internet at www.arcadiapublishing.com

An exterior view of John E. Worthen Arena, named after the Ball State president who served from 1984–2000. This spacious multi-purpose facility is an important part of the Muncie skyline.

Contents

Acknowledgments 6

Introduction 7

1. The Origins and Growth of a Program
Orville Sink, Frank Graham, Billy Williams, and Paul Parker, 1918–1930 9

2. From Bloomington to Muncie and Back Again
Branch McCracken, 1930–1938 23

3. Ups and Downs and a Trio of Coaches
Pete Phillips, Dick Stealy, and Bob Primmer, 1938–1954 33

4. The Last Faculty Member Men's Coaches
Jim Hinga and Bud Getchell, 1954–1972 45

5. Into the Mid-American Conference
Jim Holstein, Steve Yoder, and Al Brown, 1972–1987 65

6. NCAA Dreams and Nightmares
Rick Majerus and Dick Hunsaker, 1987–1993 89

7. A Rescue Mission and a Former Assistant Coach Returns
Ray McCallum and Tim Buckley, 1993–2003 107

8. Service to Ball State's Men's Basketball 122

Epilogue 124

Appendix A 125

Appendix B 128

Acknowledgments

We wish to thank several people without whose gracious assistance this book would not have been possible. Joe Hernandez, Robin Brown, and the students who work in Ball State's Athletics Communication Office gathered pictures and data for our use in a timely manner. The Ball State Photo Services staff made copies for us during one of their busiest times of the year. Ball State colleagues John Reno, Ed Shipley, Tom Dobbs, and Dave Land provided insights into the men's basketball program and some invaluable photographs. Arcadia authors Bruce Geelhoed and John Ginter were always willing to share their experiences about researching and writing books on Ball State football and baseball, respectively. Men's basketball trainer Tony Cox provided some excellent background material about teams during the last two decades. Head men's coach Tim Buckley was generous with his time in responding to questions about the current men's program and gave us contacts to obtain the photographs of the Cardinals' surprising performance in the 2001 Maui Invitational since the university does not have any pictures of this notable accomplishment. Deann Crisp, secretary extraordinaire, helped us put all of the narrative material together—several times!! John Straw and the staff in Ball State's Bracken Library archives helped us use the collection of Ball State yearbooks and other material. Jeni Sumawati helped immensely by scanning all of the photographs, while student assistants Lori Sammons and Calli Jenkins helped with cutting, pasting, and photocopying, as did history department secretary Juneyeta Gates. Honors student and English major Lydia Storie served superbly as proofreader and fact checker at the page proof stage. Finally, we want to acknowledge a special debt to retired Sports Information Director Earl Yestingsmeier, who took time over the years to keep copies of a treasure trove of source materials. Without his sense of history, books like this could not be completed.

For the information of our readers, C. Warren Vander Hill worked on the sections from Bud Getchell to the present, a period during which he knew several of the coaches and players and, for a time in the 1970s, was the Cardinals' radio color commentator. He also wished to avoid writing about the late 1950s to early 1960s because he played on Hope College teams that were 2–0 against Ball State in that period. Anthony O. Edmonds co-authored the most recent history of Ball State (Indiana University Press, 2001). He wrote this book's introduction and the chapters from 1918 through the resignation of Jim Hinga in 1968.

The authors respectfully dedicate this book to all Ball State men's basketball players, but especially to those who earned a baccalaureate degree and know what the phrase "student-athlete" really means.

Any errors of fact or interpretation are, of course, ours.

C. Warren Vander Hill
Anthony O. Edmonds

INTRODUCTION

"If the citizens of the Hoosier state were forced to choose between the continued existence of basketball and the continued existence of Western Civilization as we know it, there is little doubt as to what their choice would be."

Anon.

Since basketball is surely the national sport of Indiana, it is hardly surprising that Ball State University has fielded a men's team since its first year as a state-supported institution of higher education. From 1918–1919, when faculty member Orville Sink coached his "Normal" boys in "a few games with some local independent and high school teams and a few games with teams from other colleges," to 2002–2003, when coach Tim Buckley led the Cardinals in a full schedule of Mid-American Conference games as well as non-conference contests against perennial basketball powerhouses like Xavier and Indiana, men's basketball teams at Ball State have played squads from other institutions of higher education.

In this small work, we want to focus on some of those teams and their players and coaches. This is primarily a visual excursion into the history of Ball State men's basketball, with over 200 captioned photographs. We also include some narrative descriptions of "who," "what," "when," and "where." However, we are professional historians who have been trained to ask "how" and "why" as well. Thus, we do propose a modest thesis: throughout much of its history—from 1918 to the early 1970s—intercollegiate sports simply were not very much emphasized at Ball State. Indeed, in his doctoral dissertation on Ball State athletics from 1918–1967, Dr. Marvin Gray concludes that Ball State administrators "in general . . . supported the philosophy of `athletics for all' that was common at Ball State." Coaches of intercollegiate teams were also faculty members, positions they could retain when their coaching positions ended or were terminated. In an unpublished history of the Institution, English professor Charles Van Cleve notes that "no administrator at Ball State insisted that a man's tenure in [the department of] physical education depend on his success as a coach." They were teachers first, coaches second. Many of these coaches had Ball State connections before they began coaching. Intramural and other recreational sports shared the spotlight with, and sometimes overshadowed, intercollegiate athletics.

This pattern changed in the 1970s when Ball State hired Dave McClain as its football coach and Jim Holstein in men's basketball—non-faculty members with no previous institutional connection to Ball State. They were hired because the university wanted excellent coaches who could take Ball State to a higher level of intercollegiate athletic success, including a greater regional and even national recognition. Moreover, the decades after 1970 saw a gradual decline in the amount of press attention to intramural sports. And perhaps most importantly, in 1973, Ball State was admitted to the Mid-American Conference as its 10th member, joining institutions of similar size and mission in what became known as a "mid-major" conference.

This new approach mirrored broader changes in the institution, as Ball State in 1965 left the dwindling ranks of teachers colleges and gained university status. Although it has spent a number of years trying to figure out exactly what that status means, in general the university has sought to expand its curricular programs far beyond teacher education, recruit faculty from a national base, and increase research productivity. In other words, it has wanted to become a "real" university. And, of course, important universities have recognized athletic programs, which, in Indiana, mainly means basketball.

After some fits and starts, men's basketball in the university era certainly did bring Ball State national recognition in the late 1980s and early 1990s. Indeed, between 1987–88 and 2001–2002, the Cardinal hoopsters did not experience a losing season, won or tied for the MAC Championship six times, and played in nine national post-season tournaments. While such success was in many ways a great boon for Ball State, it also raised some interesting questions about the place of "big-time" athletics at an institution that is not a major flagship university. These questions are still being discussed as Ball State tries to compete at a high level while facing substantial deficits in its budget for intercollegiate athletics.

The men's basketball program has played an important and changing role in the history of Ball State. Reflecting the growth of the institution as a whole, it has developed from a small local program into one that often receives national attention. Moreover, it has provided hundreds of students the chance to participate and thousands of fans with moments of heartbreak and exhilaration, which, of course, is what college athletics should be all about. This is the story of men's intercollegiate basketball at Ball State University.

Before becoming a state institution, Ball State went through several incarnations, including Muncie National Institute. Here a group of MNI students practice basketball on the lawn of the institute's only building some time during the 1915-16 school year.

One

The Origins and Growth of a Program

Orville Sink, Frank Graham, Billy Williams, and Paul Parker

1918–1930

The institution that was to become Ball State University had a banner year in 1918. That spring the Board of Trustees of the Indiana State Normal School in Terre Haute agreed to accept the gift of property and a building that had been the Muncie National Institute (MNI). Purchased by members of the Ball family, powerful local industrialists, when it failed, the MNI was the last in a series of private teacher training schools ("normals") on the Muncie site. Indiana State Normal agreed to open an "Eastern Division" on the property donated to the state by the Balls. That fall, 230 students enrolled at the new institution, and Indiana State Normal School, Eastern Branch's (ISNS-EB) first men's basketball team was organized, essentially as a club that challenged other Muncie clubs and a few Indiana colleges. The 1919-20 team played eight games, all against local non-college squads, and the 1920-21 team did not even have a coach on the day it was organized. In 1921 the athletic teams adopted the rather ludicrous nickname, "Hoosieroons."

By the end of the 1920s, ISNS-EB had become Ball College, then Ball State Teachers College, independent of Terre Haute, and men's basketball was a popular and integral part of Ball State's overall athletic program. The team played a regular schedule against other colleges, including several outside of Indiana, and had achieved a level of stability in its coaching staff. Its nickname was changed from "Hoosieroons" to the more collegiate sounding "Cardinals." Most significantly, in 1923 it became a charter member of the Indiana Collegiate Conference (ICC).

The physical plant for athletics also improved markedly. In its first few seasons, the team played and practiced in venues off campus, including the local YMCA and Campbell Auditorium. But in 1922 the Ball family donated money to construct a gymnasium that still bears their name. Ball Gym became the home of Ball State basketball from 1924–1963.

In addition to all these signs of growth and regularization, the Normals-Hoosieroons-Cardinals had an overall winning record. There were some disappointing seasons—1–4 in 1920–21, 4–9 in 1923–24—and some mediocre ones—8–9 in 1925–26, 8–8 in 1928–29. However, there were also some especially fine teams in 1926–27 (13–5) and 1927–28 (17–7) under Coach Paul Parker. Parker's Cardinals won the inaugural ICC tournament in 1927–28, defeating Central Normal, Huntington, and, in the finals, North Manchester. The previous season Parker's team compiled a winning percentage of .720, a record that stood for eleven seasons.

Perhaps the most symbolically important victory came in 1925–26 against Indiana State Normal School at Terre Haute. In 1924, the Eastern Branch had become Ball Teachers College, with a separate president and budget from Terre Haute. Moreover, the Eastern Branch had never defeated the normal school from which it had just partially seceded. The Hoosieroons not only beat the Terre Haute squad; they crushed them, 51–26, before the largest crowd ever to see the team play.

By the onset of the Depression, then, we can argue that both the college and its basketball team had made significant progress. In the next eight years, under Coach Branch McCracken, the team was to reach new heights, no doubt helping the college cope with the strains brought on by economic hard times.

The first official basketball team at Ball State is seen here in 1918. The exact nature of the schedule is lost in the fog of time, but student manager Harry Fortney was able to arrange a few games against teams from local colleges. The results are unknown, although the yearbook admitted that the squad "did not win many of its games." From left to right: (front row) Brubaker, Fortney, Howell, and Lennington; (back row) Scudder, England, Williams, Pessinger, Harding, and Coach Orville Sink.

Indiana State Normal School, Eastern Branch's second basketball team was again coached by faculty member Orville Sink. According to the college yearbook, the squad was "never regularly organized, never officially recognized, never fully appreciated, and seldom loyally supported." The Normals won six of eight games in an industrial league sponsored by the local YMCA. From left to right: (seated, front row) Aaron Belcher, Coach Sink, and Noel Ware; (standing, back row) Nelson Snider, Ernest Durr, Lowell H. Neese, and Theodore Bragg.

Frank Graham, a new Professor of Chemistry and Physics, coached the Eastern Branch team in 1921–22 after Professor Sink stepped down.

Team photograph from 1920–21. The 1920-21 season began on an ambiguous note. According to the yearbook, "about 15 men" answered the first call for basketball players. Unfortunately, no coach appeared! The players convinced Graham, a new faculty member and "good-natured and experienced in the ways of basket ball," to take the helm. The season was not successful, as the team lost four of five games. Significantly, this was the first year that all contests were played against other institutions of higher education (including a 38-14 loss to Indiana Dental College and a 27-23 victory over Manchester College). From left to right: (stretched out) Nelson Snider and Shelby Caldwell; (seated, second row) Oris Shanks, Coach Graham, and an unidentified player; (standing, third row) Ralph Rigdon, Verne Flint, Glendon Rightsell, Allen Henry, and Basil Swinford.

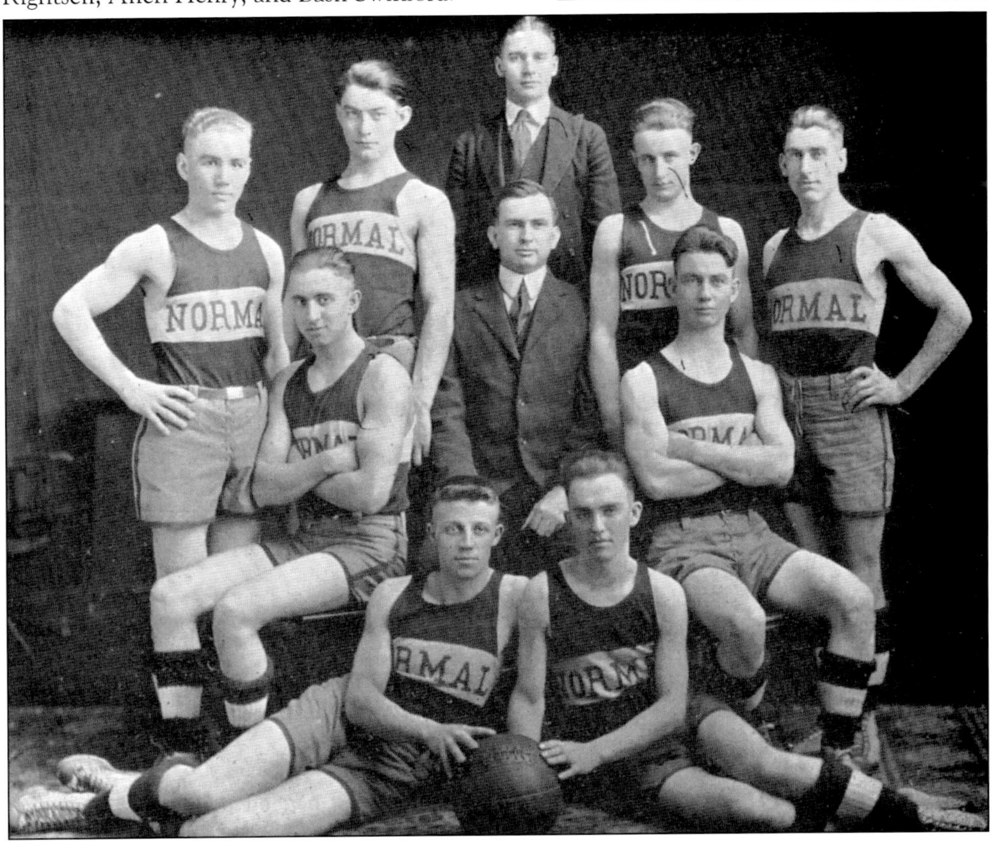

Billy Williams was the founding father of Ball State's intercollegiate athletic program and Director of Athletics and Head of Physical Education from 1921 through 1958. In 1921, he replaced Frank V. Graham as head basketball coach, a position he held until 1925. (He also coached for part of the 1929-30 season.) Although he lost his first game to Indiana Dental, 15–10, in his last game in 1930, his squad eked out a victory over Indianapolis, 34–30. His record was a lackluster 27–29–1. However, in the mid-1920s he did spearhead the successful effort to change Ball State's nickname from Hoosieroons to Cardinals. Williams was selected as a charter member of the Ball State Athletics Hall of Fame in 1976.

David Henry was the leading scorer on the 1921-22 team, tossing in 98 points in 13 games. He was especially effective when he played guard against teams with relatively weak defenses. Unfortunately, according to the yearbook, his performances were "erratic" because "he was not in condition for much of the season." Perhaps this fact helps account for the team's rather indifferent 6-7 record.

Oris Shanks, who graduated in 1924, played for the Hoosieroons for three years, 1919–20, 1922–23, and 1923–24 (although for some reason he does not appear in the 1919-20 team picture). He was the team's leading scorer each year he played and the captain of the 1923-24 team. Described by the yearbook as "clean, aggressive, and an excellent director of play," Shanks led the 1922-23 team to the college's second winning season, 9–6–1.

Campbell Auditorium was the venue for most of the Hoosieroons' games prior to the completion of Ball Gymnasium in December 1924. Located on the east side of Broadway Avenue in central Muncie, the auditorium was a multipurpose building but used mainly for roller-skating.

Taken shortly before Ball Gym was completed in late 1924, this photograph shows the large floor. At 90x175 feet, it allowed six different teams to practice simultaneously. The new gymnasium was financed by donations from the Ball family and included classrooms for physical education instruction. The construction of the gym so energized Edmund Burke Ball that he "was known to join the . . . crews at 5:00 a.m. and assist them in their day's work."

An external view of Ball Gym. The first game in the new facility was played against Franklin College on December 18, 1924, with the Hoosieroons losing badly, 40–19. The building's "collegiate Gothic" design was based on that of the University of Chicago, whose buildings deeply impressed a college building committee chaired by Frank C. Ball.

Paul Parker came to Ball State in the summer of 1925 as an Assistant Professor of Physical Education. He had played center for Indiana University and served as team captain in 1924–25. Parker took over as head basketball coach for the 1925-26 season.

The members of the 1925-26 team are not identified in this yearbook photograph. The team played poorly at first, losing its initial three contests by a combined total of 64 points, but it improved markedly, winning seven of its final twelve contests. The most notable victory came when the Hoosieroons "laid away" the Indiana Pharmacy School, 77–22.

Unidentified "yell leaders" from the 1925-26 season assume inspirational positions.

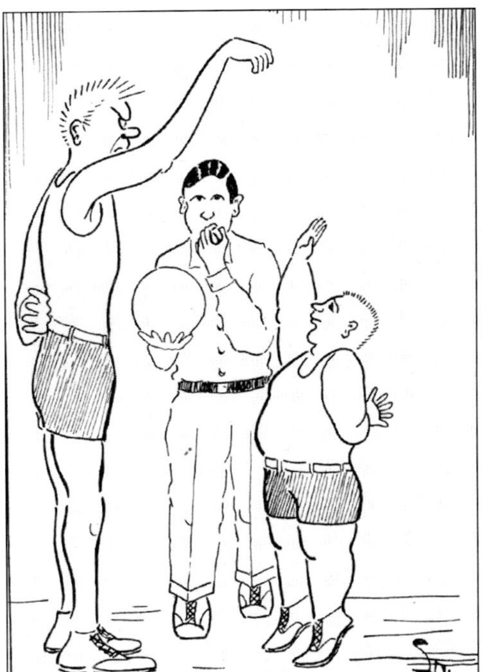

(*above*) A yearbook cartoonist known simply as "Snider" provides a humorous drawing for the basketball section of the 1926-27 annual.

(*right*) This mascot from the 1926-27 season remains unidentified. No one seems to know who he was or why he was there. His first and only appearance was in the 1926-27 yearbook.

This photograph shows the beginning of an unidentified game from the highly successful 1926-27 season, as a large crowd fills Ball Gymnasium. Coach Paul Parker's Hoosieroons went 13–5 for Ball Teachers College's best record to that point.

A tip off during one of the Cardinals' victories in the first Indiana Intercollegiate Conference tournament held at Ball Gym in 1927–28. The Cardinals won three games to emerge as champions.

Playing for the first time as a "Cardinal" rather than a "Hoosieroon," Moulton Fulmer, who earned four letters between 1926 and 1929, led the 1927-28 Ball Teachers College team to its most victories in history to that point—17—with only 7 losses. Fulmer was inducted into the Ball State Athletics Hall of Fame in 1977.

Assistant Coach Virgil Schooler, Instructor of Physical Education, temporarily replaced Paul Parker as head coach during 1928-29 season when Parker left the Muncie college to pursue graduate work at Columbia University.

The 1928-29 team under the Parker/Schooler regime finished 8–8. The players are not identified in the yearbook photograph. Among the most painful defeats was a 26-24 first-round loss to Vincennes in the ICC tournament.

The 1929-30 Cardinals bounced back from a mediocre season to win 9 of 14 games, including a 40-8 away victory at Evansville, in which the Cards held the Aces to one field goal for the entire game. Coach Parker left his position in late January 1930, to be replaced by Billy Williams, who led the team to four victories in their last five games. The players are not identified in the yearbook photograph.

From left, this trio of Ralph Heifner, David Craig, and Alvin Shumm played for the Hoosieroons in the mid-1920s.

This photograph of Branch McCracken was taken during his first year as coach of the Cardinal basketball team.

Two

FROM BLOOMINGTON TO MUNCIE AND BACK AGAIN

Branch McCracken

1930–1938

The years 1930–38 mark the first identifiable "era" in Ball State basketball history largely because of the impact of one man, Coach Branch McCracken. He was hired in the spring of 1930 to replace Paul Parker, who stayed at Columbia to pursue a graduate degree. McCracken had been a star player at Indiana University, earning consensus All-America honors as a senior in 1929–1930 and setting the Western Conference (later to become the Big Ten) scoring record that year. After a brief stint playing semi-professional ball, McCracken came to Ball State determined to create a winning team.

His biographer describes him as "a ferocious and complete competitor." The 6'4" McCracken was known to his IU teammates as "Big Bear" because of "his size and his tendency to scowl." John Lewellen, who played guard for McCracken in 1935–36, recalls sitting next to the coach during games. When McCracken got excessively excited, he wouldn't jump up and down, yelling and screaming: "He'd just grab my thigh and squeeze so hard," Lewellen remembers, "that I'd almost scream." Branch McCracken thus brought an intense dedication and determination to coaching at Ball State, as he compiled a 93-41 record in his eight years at the helm.

No doubt his best-remembered and most important game came in December 1937 when McCracken's Cardinals stunned his alma mater, Indiana University, 42–38. Ball State had lost three straight games to their downstate rivals in the previous three seasons and was the clear underdog in this fourth contest. It seemed that the underdog status was richly deserved when the Cards were down 30–23 midway through the 2nd half. But led by guards Rex Rudicel and Ray Lackey (who each scored a game high 13 points), Ball State pulled ahead 38–36. Then Rudicel and Lackey used their ball handling skills to slow the game down, resulting in the four-point victory. The local *Muncie Star* positively beamed with community pride, referring glowingly to the "spectacular upset" in this "history-making win." No doubt in part because of this victory, IU successfully courted McCracken, who left Ball State the next year to begin his legendary 26-year coaching career with the "Hurryin'" Hoosiers. (He took a bit of Ball State with him, however, marrying the daughter of the college's president, Lemuel Pittenger. According to one report, Miss Pittenger said on first viewing the tall, handsome young coach, "That's the man I'm going to marry.")

McCracken's tenure at Ball State coincided with the heart of the Great Depression, but the kind of success that the basketball Cards experienced no doubt helped cushion students, staff, and friends of the college from some of its psychological trauma. Emblematic of the good feelings generated by the team is the hymn of praise sung by the yearbook commenting on the victory over IU: "In the battle of the ages . . . , [t]he Redbirds had umph and eezil to spare as they . . . raced the Bloomington netters into the boards for a memorable . . . victory that will be talked of as long as Ball Brothers make fruit jars. It was the blue ribbon athletic achievement of Ball State's Cardinals, this or any other year." Such was the power of college hoops in dark Depression days.

The players in the 1930-31 squad are not identified in this yearbook photograph. At 9–5, the team matched the record of the previous season. After winning six of their first seven games, the Cardinals hit a rough stretch at the end of the season. The fact that two of the losses were by the scores of 15–14 and 15–12 suggest a certain lack of offensive punch.

This team photograph of the 1931-32 squad features Coach McCracken in the middle of the back row, obviously taller than members of his team. A look at the player to the immediate right of the coach suggests that the equipment manager must have run out of Cards jerseys. Players are not identified in this yearbook photograph.

Waiting for the center jump in one of the games played in 1931–32. The team went 9–7 with impressive wins over old rival Indiana State and Western State College (later to become Western Michigan), new to the schedule.

Unidentified yell leaders from the 1931-32 season practice their moves.

The 1933-34 team experienced a losing season, going 9–10. According to a cryptic comment in the yearbook, part of the difficulty may have been that "McCracken was faced with a disciplinary problem and was forced to adjust a new starting line-up." There were no details. Curiously, no letters were awarded in basketball that year either. The players are not identified in this yearbook photograph.

This action is from a game during the 1934-35 season. The team managed to go 9–9, the highlight being two easy victories over traditional rival Earlham.

John Lewellen started at guard for the 1934-35 Cards but left the team the next season in order to concentrate on swimming and diving. He also won national acclaim as a javelin thrower, setting the Ball State record. He joined the Ball State physical education staff in 1937 and served in a number of coaching capacities, including tennis, cross-country, golf, swimming, and football. He retired as Director of Aquatics and was inducted into the Ball State Athletics Hall of Fame in 1978.

Mel Wilson played for the Cardinal hoopsters for three seasons (1933–35) as well as for the Ball State football team. He also earned three letters in track. In basketball, he was starting center for Coach McCracken and one of the team's leading scorers. After graduation, he had a successful career in high school coaching, concentrating on track and field. He was inducted into the Ball State Athletics Hall of Fame in 1978.

Cardinal center Forrest Shook is seen here in a center jump during the game against Indiana University in December 1935. Although Ball State lost to the Hoosiers in Bloomington, 44–28, the Cards went on to compile a fine 13-7 record—the best to that point in McCracken's career. After the regular season ended, Ball State fashioned a 33-17 blow out of Wayne University in the pre-district Olympic trials, before losing in the district trials to Central Normal, 46–23.

Guard Max Rudicel starts the ball up court in a game from the 1936-37 season in which the Cards went 13–6. A challenging schedule included the continuing rivalry with Indiana University and Western State College, as well as the first-ever meeting between the Cardinals and the Badgers of Wisconsin (all of which Ball State lost). Victories against traditional rivals Indiana State (35–25 and 43–30) and Wabash (38–30 and 33–25) were high points.

This is the program cover for the 1937 Ball State-IU game.

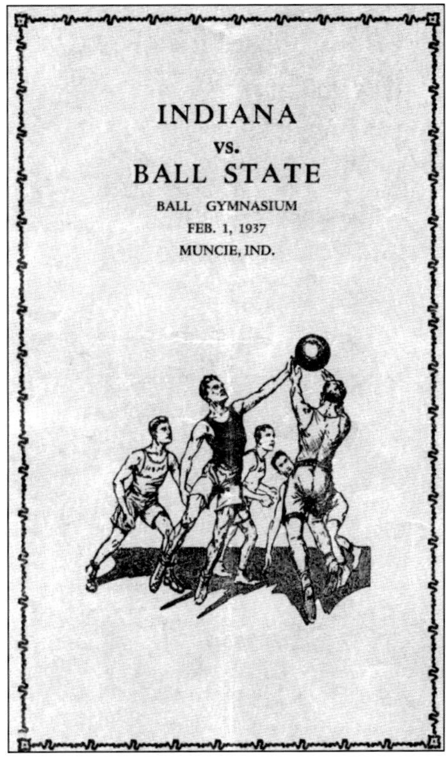
INDIANA
vs.
BALL STATE
BALL GYMNASIUM
FEB. 1, 1937
MUNCIE, IND.

An unidentified IU player controls the ball in the Cardinal-Hoosier game in February 1937. According to the yearbook, "McCracken's lads [were] as nervous as a freshman at a sorority tea" and "experienced scurvy bombing luck and canned but 12 per cent of their tries." Things would be different in the game against Indiana the next season.

The 1934-35 freshman basketball team, coached by Billy Williams, was Ball State's first undefeated freshman squad. The individuals are not identified in this yearbook photograph. Players from this team, like Rex and Max Rudicel and Harry Casterline, became the nucleus of McCracken's immensely successful varsity teams over the next three seasons (43–17). Ball State's basketball program included a freshman or junior varsity team until 1976. These teams gave a few more student athletes the opportunity to play intercollegiate basketball, very much in line with the "athletics for all" philosophy that Ball State subscribed to for many years. The university eliminated these teams after the 1976 season.

Cold Card fans wait to board a coach for an away game at Indiana Central in January 1937.

The 1937-38 team was one of the best in Ball State basketball history. Led by a core of veterans from the undefeated 1934-35 freshman team, the Cardinals won 17 of 21 games. After opening losses to powerhouse Notre Dame and always tough Indiana Central, the Cards stunned Indiana University in one of the great Ball State victories. (Unfortunately, there are no identifiable action pictures of the victory against IU in the yearbook, local newspapers, or the Ball State Archives.) After losses to Franklin (by a point) and a strong Toledo team in early January, the Cardinals won their last 13 games, including "revenge" victories against Indiana Central and Franklin. It was a team for the ages. From left to right: (front row) Casterline, Boyd, and Lackey; (second row) Hole, R. Rudicel, Stout, Gardner, and Bundy; (third row) Johnson, R. Risinger, Shook, J. Risinger, and Doering.

Rex Rudicel, the diminutive guard (5'5") and brother of teammate Max, has become a Ball State legend. Nicknamed "the Phantom Bantam," Rudicel was a regular on the Cardinal basketball team from 1936–38. He was selected to the Little All-State Team as a sophomore and the Big All-State Team as a senior. He played one year for the Indianapolis professional team in the National Basketball League. In 1948, he was named head basketball coach at Burris, the teaching laboratory school for Ball State, a position he held for 22 seasons. Rudicel was inducted into the Ball State Athletics Hall of Fame in 1977.

Three

Ups and Downs and a Trio of Coaches

Pete Phillips, Dick Stealy, and Bob Primmer

1938–1954

Although Ball State lost a great coach when Branch McCracken went to Indiana in 1938, over the next fifteen seasons his successors did manage a winning record—barely, at 128–126. In only five of those seasons did the Cardinals post more victories than defeats.

No doubt this uneven record was partly the result of the dislocations caused by World War II. Ball State saw its male enrollment drop from 694 in 1940–41 to 117 in 1943–44, when, in fact, the college actually cancelled its basketball season. (Other institutions must have had worse problems, however, since Ball State rolled to one of its best seasons in history in 1944–45 at 10–3—and that with only 136 men enrolled!)

Part of the difficulty, however, may also have been the fact that building high-powered intercollegiate athletic teams was not a major institutional priority. Ball State still seemed wedded to the idea of "athletics for all," with intercollegiate teams serving primarily as an "educational experience" for the participants. As John R. Emens, president of Ball State from 1945–1968, argued, education was "the sum total of one's experience." Therefore, he saw intercollegiate athletics, including basketball, as "just one part of the physical education curriculum, just as the band is an outgrowth of the music curriculum."

The three men who coached the Cardinals from 1938–1954 certainly fit well into this philosophy. Pete Phillips (1938–48), Dick Stealy (1948–52), and Bob Primmer (1952–54) all became faculty members in the department of physical education. They were teacher-coaches, not just coaches. And when they stepped down from their coaching positions, they all remained on the faculty until they retired.

Although intercollegiate sports were hardly over-emphasized during this period, Ball State did see the need to remain part of a conference. In 1950, the old Indiana Intercollegiate Conference, which had included most Indiana public and private colleges in its membership, disbanded. A new, smaller conference—the Indiana Collegiate Conference (ICC)—was formed. Ball State, along with Butler, Evansville, Indiana State, St. Joseph's, and Valparaiso become charter members, and DePauw joined in 1953. Significantly, Ball State's record in the first four years of conference play was mediocre—16–24—reflecting the team's overall losing record during those four seasons.

But there were some bright spots in this decade and a half. Pete Phillips's 1944-45 team achieved the second best winning percentage (.770) in Ball State basketball history. Phillips also led winning teams in three of the last four seasons he coached. Dick Stealy's 1948-49 team went 12–6, winning eight of their last nine games. Bob Primmer's losing season in 1953–54 saw a stellar performance by Stan Davis, who led the ICC in rebounding with 144 and was selected to the all-conference team.

Overall, however, the basketball Cardinals mainly tread water in this period, especially when contrasted to the Branch McCracken years. In fact, with the exception of three splendid seasons under Coach Jim Hinga (1954–68), this trend would continue, and even worsen, over the next twenty years.

Ardith "Pete" Phillips replaced Branch McCracken as head coach in 1938. As the yearbook quipped, after departing "for greener pastures, about the only experienced men McCracken had left for Philips was manager Lloyd Biberstine." A 1920 graduate of Indiana University, where he earned three letters in basketball and captained the 1919-20 team, Phillips coached on the high school level from 1921–38.

A Ball State player attempts a free throw against Toledo during the 1938-39 season, illustrating the classic underhand style common in this time period. We don't know if he made the toss, but if he did, it provided the winning margin in a 42-41 victory.

Roy Gardner played guard for Ball State in 1938–39 and 1939–40. Nicknamed the "Lawrenceburg Lilliputian" (based on his home town and size), Gardner led the squad in scoring in 1939–40 as Pete Phillips's Cardinals compiled an impressive 12-6 record. After graduation, he became a successful high school coach in basketball and golf, mainly at Batesville. But he is best remembered for his career as a referee on both the high school and college levels, including stints in Big Ten basketball and the 1967 Cotton Bowl. The Roy Gardner Memorial Award is given to the outstanding high school official in Indiana. Gardner was inducted into the Ball State Athletics Hall of Fame in 1981.

Richard (Dick) Stealy was both a player and a coach for the Cardinals. He earned three letters in basketball between 1939 and 1941, playing center for Pete Phillips's squad. (He also lettered for three years in track and football.) After service in the army, Stealy returned to Ball State where he began a successful coaching career, especially in track, leading the Cardinals to nine Indiana Collegiate Conference crowns. He served as head basketball coach from 1948 to 1952, but his teams went 36–42, with only one winning season. Stealy, who was a Professor of Physical Education as well, was elected to the Ball State Athletics Hall of Fame in 1977.

The opening tip-off in the battle between Ball State and Indiana University, at Bloomington on December 5, 1938. The Hoosiers buried the Cardinals 54–28. Indiana head coach Branch McCracken thus executed a measure of revenge on former Ball State head coach Branch McCracken!

Cardinal Bill Hale knocks down a set shot in a game against Butler during the 1942-43 season. The Cards went 7–10, losing several close games. Ball State did, however, defeat future Mid-American Conference rivals Miami of Ohio and Northern Illinois.

After the 1943-44 season was cancelled because of World War II, the Cards came back in 1944–45 to play superb basketball. Led by future hall-of-famer, forward Marvin Heaton, the Redbirds went 10–3, highlighted by a 79-20 drubbing of Anderson and a 64-36 victory over long-standing rival Butler, avenging an early season loss to the Bulldogs. From left to right: (first row) Marvin Heaton, Robert Pursley, Charles Keller, Robert Engle, James Abbott, Fred Riley; (second row) Richard Doversberger, Richard Valandingham, Michael Drake, Robert Cruse, Robert Sutton; (third row) Robert LaGarde, Robert Harris, Maurice Davis, Roger Marsh, Cyril Hall, Hugh Locke; (fourth row) student manager Philip Trees, Coach Pete Phillips.

Cardinal Fred Grimes fires a jump shot against Central Normal during the 1945-46 season. As the yearbook joyfully noted, by late 1945, Ball State had "men again." In fact, so many prospects showed up that Coach Phillips had to schedule alternating evening workouts. All the new players didn't help the team to a winning record, however, as the Cards went 7–9.

A Cardinal player with the ball draws a crowd in a game during the 1946-47 season. Some 250 prospects showed up to try out for the team in the winter of 1946, reflecting a substantial increase of males on the Muncie campus—many of them veterans of the war. Coach Phillips managed to whittle the number down to 45 before the season's opener. He fashioned the team into a winner as it compiled a 9-8 record. The most notable victory came against University of Wisconsin-Milwaukee, by a lopsided 73-42 score. The Milwaukee school went on to win the Wisconsin state college basketball championship that season.

Members of the 1947-48 team meet for an informal chat in the locker room showers. The players are not identified in this yearbook photograph. The teammates had good reason to smile as the Cards went 12–5. Led by Bob Straight and Marv Heaton, Ball State won eight of their last nine games, including victories over strong out-of-state teams from Western Michigan, Eastern Michigan, Illinois State, and Northern Illinois.

Ray Ashley played forward for Coach Pete Phillips for three seasons, 1939–41. No doubt his greatest accomplishment came in January 1940 when he scored 32 points against Franklin when Ball State defeated their in-state rivals 54–37. At the time, it was the second highest point total ever recorded in one game by a college hoopster in Indiana and remained the single-game Ball State record for nine years. Ashley coached high school sports for two years before entering the navy in 1943, after which he returned to high school coaching. In 1962, he became assistant director of alumni relations at Ball State and served for ten years as executive director of the Cardinal Varsity Club. He was inducted into the Ball State Athletics Hall of Fame in 1980.

Robert (Bob) Straight was a four-year letterman from 1947–50. He enrolled at Ball State after two years in the navy, one of several World War II veterans who played for the Cards. He was named to the Indiana College All-Star team in 1950. After graduation, Straight became one of the state's finest basketball coaches, compiling an overall record of 247–106 at four Indiana secondary schools. His 1963-64 Huntington High School team went 27–2, losing in the state finals to Lafayette Jefferson. Straight was inducted into the Ball State Athletics Hall of Fame in 1979.

In 1948, Dick Stealy replaced Pete Phillips as head coach when Phillips stepped down. According to the yearbook, Phillips wanted "to spend his time and efforts developing freshman prospects." Stealy was a star player for the Cardinals from 1938–41.

Players from Ball State and DePauw scrap for the ball during one of their games in 1948–49. The teams split in what was a very successful season for the Cardinals. Led by forwards Marv Heaton and Floyd Reed, who combined for 619 points, Stealy's debut team went 12–6. The future looked promising.

An unidentified member of the 1949-50 Cardinal team drives to the basket. Stealy's second season was something of a disappointment, as Ball State broke even at 9–9. The high point of the season was a 69-44 thumping of Miami of Ohio. (Through the magic of comparative point differentials, the yearbook took this victory margin and with only four degrees of separation had Ball State beating Bradley, the nation's number one team, by 51 points!)

Several members the 1949-50 Cardinals met in Worthen Arena on December 11, 1999, for a 50-year reunion. From left to right are Marvin "Marv" Heaton, Dick Stealy, Bob Straight, Floyd "Orv" Reed, Max "Fred" Reed, Clyde Swackhamer, Jack Sexton, David Locke, Bill McCarter, and, doing battle with the Ball State mascot Charlie Cardinal, Phil McCarter.

Marvin (Marv) Heaton is the only Ball State basketball player to receive five varsity letters in the sport. Because of the exigencies of World War II, the college did not count the 1944-45 season against his eligibility. After two years in the Army, Heaton started for the Cards for the next four seasons. He was a prolific scorer, with his 1,186-point total placing him 17th on the list of Ball State's career scoring leaders. His 34 points against St. Joseph's during the 1948-49 campaign was a Ball State record at the time. After graduation, Heaton entered a career of high school coaching and teaching, primarily at Richmond High School. He was elected to the Ball State Athletics Hall of Fame in 1983.

Cardinal freshman Jack Cross drives for a breakaway lay-up during a game in the 1952-53 season. Ball State improved to 9–9 during Coach Bob Primmer's first year. Cross was a four-year letterman (1952–55), led the team in scoring in his sophomore and junior years, and made the all-conference team in 1953 and 1954. After graduation, he became a successful high school basketball coach and educator. He was inducted into the Ball State Athletics Hall of Fame in 1980.

Bob Primmer replaced Dick Stealy as head coach in 1952. He played varsity basketball at Franklin College in the early 1930s, after which he coached on the high school level, primarily at South Bend Central. He stepped down as Cardinal basketball coach after only two seasons because of ill health. He worked as coordinator of financial aid and student employment from 1955–1958, when he succeeded Billy Williams as director of athletics, a post he held until he retired in 1970. Primmer was inducted into the Ball State Athletics Hall of Fame in 1978.

Stan Davis, the Cardinals' first African American varsity basketball player, shoots a short jumper against Wabash during the 1953-54 season. Davis's performance was a high point in an otherwise disappointing 9-12 season. He led the Cards in rebounding, averaging 6.9 per game; he also broke the Ball State single game scoring record when he tossed in 35 points against DePauw on February 10, 1954.

Four

The Last Faculty Member Men's Coaches
Jim Hinga and Bud Getchell

1954–1972

Ball State grew enormously between 1954 and 1972. Enrollment skyrocketed from 3623 to almost 20,000. More significantly, in 1965 the Indiana General Assembly changed Ball State's status from teachers college to university, reflecting growth in both enrollment and the diversity of academic programs.

In many ways, the basketball program reflected these changes. In 1956, the college joined both the National Association of Intercollegiate Athletics (NAIA) and the National Collegiate Athletic Association (NCAA). Founded in the late 1930s, the NAIA was an organization focusing on small colleges with limited emphasis on intercollegiate athletics. The NCAA, on the other hand, included divisions for both small colleges and major universities with nationally recognized athletic programs. Ball State, according to one observer, joined both to see which would be the best fit. The college dropped out of the NAIA in 1960, casting its lot with the larger, more prestigious organization. University status and booming enrollments also convinced president John R. Emens that Ball State had simply outgrown the Indiana Collegiate Conference (ICC). The university withdrew from it in June 1968. Finally, construction on the new Men's Physical Education Building was completed in 1963. The main feature of this complex was a multi-purpose gymnasium with an official seating capacity of 6,880, providing a facility worthy of a strong intercollegiate basketball program.

In a sense, however, intercollegiate basketball at Ball State still was not an institutional priority. Both of the head coaches in this period, Jim Hinga and Bud Getchell (who had been Hinga's assistant), were Ball State faculty members as well as coaches. Emens, who was president until fall 1968, maintained his vision of intercollegiate athletics as essentially one small part of the total educational experience. And, significantly, the basketball program was only intermittently successful, compiling a record that can charitably be called mediocre, with 184 wins and 236 losses, hardly an accomplishment that an institution heading for greater recognition could boast about.

And yet there were some marvelously magic moments in this period. Jim Hinga, who replaced Bob Primmer as head coach in 1954, saw his 1956-7 squad (19–8) selected to play in the 1957 National Association of Intercollegiate Athletics post-season tournament—the first national post-season appearance in Ball State basketball history. The Cardinals defeated Oakland City and Anderson in their district. In the next round in Kansas City, Ball State easily won the opening game against Troy State but lost in the next round to a taller Texas Southern squad. Moreover, Hinga's 1963-64 team had an impressive 17-8 record, including victories in its final ten regular season games. This team made Ball State's first and only appearance in the NCAA College Division post-season tournament, although it lost both its games.

But these highs points were exceptions. Coach Hinga's teams compiled losing records in 8 of his 14 years at the helm. In his last season, 1967–68, the Cardinals had a disappointing 10-12 mark, their fourth losing campaign in a row. In addition, as we have noted, 1968 marked Ball State's departure from the Indiana Collegiate Conference. This decision began a period in which the university spent a great deal of time trying to find an appropriate conference affiliation while also hoping that the well established Mid-American Conference might expand and admit the Muncie institution.

When Hinga returned to his teaching assignment on a full-time basis, his assistant, Bud Getchell, was promoted to head coach. Getchell's Cardinals featured a fast break style of play but with more emphasis on defense than had been the case with Cardinal teams of the previous decade and a half. During Getchell's four-year tenure, Ball State had some excellent individual players, most notably Jim Regenold, who set several scoring records, but his squads were never able to put together anything even close to a winning season. Opponents consisted largely of teams from the old ICC, members of the Mid-American Conference, and the four other schools in the short-lived Conference of Midwestern Universities (Midwestern Conference), which Ball State University joined as a charter member in 1969. This league, which included Northern and Southern Illinois, Indiana State, and Illinois State, in addition to Ball State, broke up in spring 1972. Perhaps the high point of Getchell's coaching career came at a December 1971 holiday tournament in Springfield, Massachusetts, where the Cardinals defeated both Boston University and Bucknell.

At the end of the 1971-72 season, Getchell chose to give up his basketball coaching duties and take up a faculty assignment in the Adult Fitness area of the university's rapidly developing Human Performance Laboratory. This decision marked the end of an era in Ball State men's basketball coaches. Up to this time, all of the Cardinal coaches were faculty members who coached, but in November 1971, Ball State was classified as a major university in men's basketball by the NCAA's Basketball Classification Committee. From this point on, all men's basketball coaches would have contractual assignments as coaches with no expectation that they be part of the physical education faculty. A new era was about to begin.

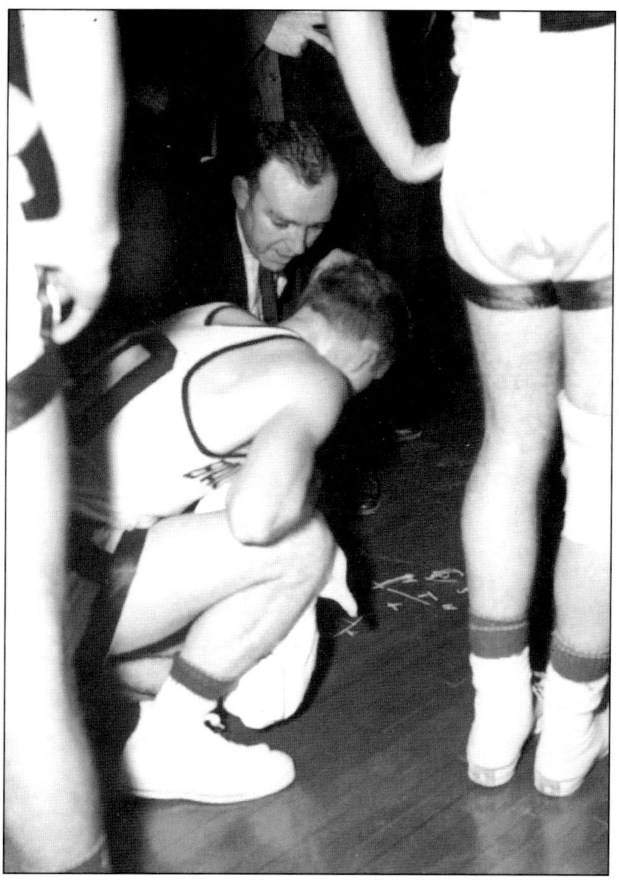

Here Coach Jim Hinga gives instructions to his team during a time-out. Hinga served as Ball State's head basketball coach from 1954–55 through 1967–68, the longest tenure of any head hoops coach in the institution's history. He was elected to the Ball State Athletics Hall of Fame in 1984.

One of Ball State's finest teams ever, the 1956-57 squad went undefeated at Ball Gym and advanced to the school's first national post-season tournament. Going around the horseshoe from the bottom left: Larry Koehl (with ball), Carl Miller, John Lebo, Bob Crawford, Ted Fullhart, Dave Skelton, Jack Lowe, Tom Dobbs, Jim Harris, Wayne Van Sickle, Terry Schurr, Jerry Banker, and Wilbur Davis. In the front middle from left to right are student managers Loren Grabner and Ken Miller. Behind them is Coach Jim Hinga.

On December 17, 2001, veterans of the 1956-57 NAIA tournament team reassembled, including, from left to right, Dave Skelton, Wilbur Davis, John Lebo, Ted Fullhart, Loren Grabner (manager), Terry Schurr, Wayne VanSickle, Jerry Banker, Coach Jim Hinga, and Tom Dobbs.

Tom Dobbs was one of Ball State's most prolific scorers. A four-year letterman, he started 84 consecutive games between 1953–54 and 1957 and set school records with 1,210 career points, 458 in one season (1956–57), and 39 in one game (versus DePauw in 1957). Dobbs made the All-Indiana Collegiate Conference team as a senior and led the 1956-57 team to the NAIA National Tournament in Kansas City. He served as assistant coach of the Cardinals from 1968 to1977 and a member of the physical education faculty from 1968 until his retirement in 1997. In 1981, he was inducted into the Ball State Athletics Hall of Fame.

Wayne Van Sickle practices his jump shot. A transfer from the University of Michigan, Van Sickle was a star player on the 1956-57 Ball State team. He was twice named to the All-ICC squad and was among the Cardinals free throw leaders of his era (1955–57). After graduation, he became a high school teacher, coach, and referee. Van Sickle was inducted into the BSU Athletics Hall of Fame in 1980.

Terry Schurr drives to the basket in a victory against Anderson in a 1957 NAIA post-season game. Schurr was once called by former Indiana Governor Otis Bowen "the finest small man I've ever seen play." (Both Bowen and Schurr are from Bremen, Indiana.) Schurr was an outstanding guard for the Cardinals from 1956–58.

Ball State fans brave the cold to welcome team members and coaches returning to Muncie from the NAIA tournament in 1957.

In a game during the 1958-59 season, Wilbur Davis battles two Evansville Aces for a rebound while Jim Sullivan (50) follows in. Davis was a rugged low post player of the late 1950s. His game featured an assortment of moves in the paint and great skill at getting a rebound and passing to start a fast break. Sullivan was a Cardinal standout of the same era.

John Kunze fires his southpaw jumper in a game against Butler during the 1960-61 season. A consistent outside scorer in the early 1960s, Kunze's most memorable game came against Evansville, then the top-ranked small college team in the country, as the Cards pulled off a stunning upset, 91–80, on January 4, 1962. Kunze scored a game-high 34 points.

Coaching clinics have always been an important part of Cardinal basketball. Here Coach Jim Hinga, second from the left, discusses the plans for a 1962 clinic with staff and guests.

Coach Jim Hinga voices his displeasure with a referee's decision during a game in the early 1960s. Players John Lee (left) and Ed Butler (right) hurry to the "rescue."

Stan Neal goes to his left and to the hoop during the 1961-62 season. Neal was one of Ball State's finest outside shooters of the early 1960s. In his senior season, he was team MVP and first team All-Indiana Collegiate Conference. In January 1965, he burned St. Joseph's for 40 points, only one example of his outstanding point production. He was later head basketball coach at Burris Laboratory School from 1970 to 1973.

Mike Readnour drives to the glass in a game in 1961–62. Readnour lettered three times in basketball (1960–62) and established the school's career rebounding record at the time, 732. After graduation, he earned his doctorate in chemistry at Purdue and taught in the chemistry department at Southeast Missouri State University. He was inducted into the Ball State Athletics Hall of Fame in 1987.

The 1963-64 Cardinals posted a 17-8 record and were selected to participate in the NCAA College Division tourney. They lost in the first round to Southern Illinois, 88–81 and to Jackson State in the consolation game, 92–71. From left to right are: (first row) Ron Galloway, Tom Barnes, Stan Neal, Curt Irvin, John Lee, and Keith Henschen; (second row) student managers George Griffith and Mel Goldman, Jerry Beguhn, Joe Hoffman, and Coach Jim Hinga; (third row) Ron Latham, Duane Hamilton, Ed Butler, Bob Heady, and Dick Reedy.

Dick Reedy leads an effective fast break down the court to score an easy lay-up for the Cardinal cause during the highly successful 1963-64 season.

Earl Yestingsmeier was a student manager for Coach Jim Hinga. During his long tenure as Ball State's sports information director (1959–1980) and men's golf coach (1962–98), he worked tirelessly to make certain that historical materials about Cardinal athletes were kept, filed, and maintained. Yestingsmeier was inducted into the Ball State Athletics Hall of Fame in 1981.

Bob Heady was a star letterman in both baseball and basketball in1963 and 1964. As a junior, his 12.7 scoring average and 7.2 rebounds per game helped lead the Card hoopsters to a 15-9 record. Although his production fell the next year because of a knee injury, Ball State still went 17–6. After graduation, Heady became a successful secondary school baseball and basketball coach, primarily at Shenandoah High School. He was elected to the Ball State Athletics Hall of Fame in 1985.

Ed Butler played for Ball State between 1962 and 1964, leading the Cardinals to an appearance in the NCAA College Division Tournament in the 1963-64 season. The most prolific rebounder in Ball State history, Butler still holds eight school records in this area, including most career rebounds (1231), most rebounds in one season (442), and most rebounds in one game (27). (Indeed, he claims the top nine rebounding games in Ball State history.) He also ranks 14th in career scoring. After graduating in 1964, he received a master's degree in urban planning and served in the Peace Corps in Ethiopia. He was inducted into the Ball State Athletics Hall of Fame in 1979.

An external and inside view of what came to be known as "men's gym." In 1963, the Cardinal men's basketball team moved from an often overcrowded Ball Gymnasium to more spacious quarters in the new Men's Physical Education Building on the north side of the campus. It was later called University Gym and renamed Irving Gym in 1990 to recognize a gift of 2.25 million dollars from the Irving Brothers Gravel Company and Irving Materials Inc. to the University's "Wings for the Future" capital campaign.

Terry Stillabower arches one from the outside during the 1966-67 season. A Cardinal stalwart of the mid-1960s, Stillabower was an amazing long-range shooter. Perhaps his "night of nights" came on January 11, 1967, when he torched arch-rival Indiana State for 40 points on 20 field goals, still a Cardinal record for most field goals in a single game.

Mack Sawyer drives for a lay up against Bowling Green in an 87-70 loss in the 1967-68 season. In the mid-1960s, Sawyer was a leading scorer and rebounder for Coach Hinga. Selected team most valuable player in 1965–66 and 1966–67, he is still listed among the Cardinals' all-time rebounding leaders.

John Lee, a former New Castle High School standout, played for Jim Hinga's Cardinals for three seasons. A fine outside shooter and battler under the basket, Lee, along with center Ed Butler, led Ball State to its only appearance in the NCAA College-level post-season tourney.

John Miller was a backcourt standout from 1966–68. An unselfish player, he was a team leader in assists and contributed outside scoring as well.

Leroy "Bud" Getchell, a native of Springfield, Massachusetts, was a star athlete at Springfield College. He joined the BSU Physical Education faculty in the late 1950s and completed a doctorate at the University of Illinois in 1965. Getchell was freshman coach and an assistant to Jim Hinga before being named head coach in 1968. During his four-year stint directing the Cardinal hoop fortunes, he compiled a 30-67 won-lost record. A tenured faculty member, Getchell turned his interests to the emerging Adult Physical Fitness field after he gave up coaching and became nationally recognized for his writing and research in this area.

Steve Ricks shoots from the side. Ricks was a key inside player for Coach Bud Getchell in the mid-1960s. He led the Cardinals in rebounding in 1967–68.

Gary Miller releases a jump shot. Miller was a junior college All-America at Brevard (Florida) Junior College before transferring to Ball State in the mid-1960s. He was one of BSU's leading scorers and rebounders during his two years with the Cardinals. He was team MVP for the 1968-69 season.

Barry Kennedy looks for a passing opportunity on the inside. An excellent passer and outside shooter, Kennedy was backcourt leader for the Cardinals in the late 1960s.

Marty Miggenberg (*left*), a rugged inside player for the Cardinals in the late 1960s, was a skilled rebounder and shooter.

Roger Law (*below*) briefly out of action with an injury. A hard-nosed guard in the early 1970s, Law was an excellent passer and outside shooter.

Bill Clark (*left*), a 6'-7" center, was a leading scorer and rebounder from 1971 to 1973.

Marzine Moore was a skilled shooter and rebounder for BSU teams in the late 1960s. Moore was a crowd favorite with his assortment of low post and perimeter moves.

Mike Holland works off the low post. Holland was a premier scorer and rebounder for coach Bud Getchell's teams of the late 1960s. He was named team MVP in both 1968–69 (with Gary Miller) and 1969–70. He shares the record for best season field goal percentage, 60 percent in 1969–70.

Jim Regenold joined the Cards as a highly recruited scorer from nearby Anderson. His Ball State career certainly lived up to advanced billing. From 1969–72, he rewrote the scoring record book. He averaged 27.5 points per game in 1970–71 and finished his career with 1,685 total points on an assortment of long-range jumpers, determined drives to the iron, and deadly free-throw accuracy. He was elected to the BSU Athletics Hall of Fame in 1983.

Five

INTO THE MID-AMERICAN CONFERENCE

Jim Holstein, Steve Yoder, and Al Brown

1972–1987

Jim Holstein, a successful small college coach at Indiana's St. Joseph's College, was selected to be the Cardinals' first full-time men's basketball coach. He took over for the 1972-73 season, which saw the team continue its losing ways, finishing 9–15.

However, three months after the Cardinals' ninth straight losing season, the university was finally admitted to the Mid-American Conference, something Ball State had sought for several years. The university became the tenth member of one of the nation's most respected athletic and academic conferences. Even though the men's basketball team would not play a full MAC schedule until 1975–76, the pressure was certainly on Holstein to recruit players who could complete with such MAC basketball powers as Miami, Bowling Green, and Toledo.

From 1973 to 1976, Holstein and his staff attempted to recruit at that level, something new for the program. He had some measure of success, especially in attracting Indiana All-Star Larry Bullington, who set numerous records during his varsity years; 6'10" center Randy Boarden; football star Shafer Suggs; and backcourt scorers Jim Fields and Kim Kaufman. Although Holstein's teams posted some solid victories, defeating both Cincinnati and Ohio State in Muncie, his record against MAC opponents was lackluster; by the 1976-77 season, he had managed only one winning season, 14–12, in 1973–74. Shortly before the end of the 1976-77 campaign, Holstein submitted his resignation, and the quest to find a new head mentor who would produce teams that could compete for the MAC championship began again. Holstein's main complaint about what he was asked to do for the Cardinals' program may be summed up in one statement he made to an assistant coach: "You can't have a champagne program on a beer budget."

This time around the Cardinals stayed in-house and named Steve Yoder, who had been an assistant coach for Holstein during the 1976-77 season. As the new men's head coach, Yoder had the reputation of being a solid teacher of the game, as well as a skilled recruiter. The Plymouth, Indiana, native also had many contacts with high school coaches, something that the Cardinal faithful hoped would pay off in the recruiting wars.

Yoder's first season continued the losing pattern (10–15 overall, 6–6 MAC), but with Illinois high school star Mike Drews, a consistent scoring threat, and a more mature Randy Boarden, the Cardinals improved to 16–11 and 9–7 in the MAC the following year. Yoder's most important decision in 1979, however, was to sign Muncie Central High School star Ray McCallum, a player he had not originally recruited. A 5'-9" shooting guard, McCallum had a successful career with the high school champion Bearcats but had been overlooked in recruiting by virtually all of the Division I programs in the Midwest. McCallum joined the Cardinals as a real question mark, largely due to his size. However, over the next four years, he rewrote the Cardinal record books in several categories, became one of the most popular players in Ball State history in any sport, led the team to its first MAC Tournament Championship (1980–81) and on to its first appearance in the NCAA Division I Tournament, where they lost a heartbreaker in the first round to Boston College, 93–90.

Yoder surrounded McCallum with an able supporting cast, which included inside post player George Bradley and the talented John Williams. The following year, 1981–82, the Cardinals again led by McCallum and Williams, finished the campaign with a 17-11 record and won the MAC going 12–4. They lost to Northern Illinois in the MAC tourney final and were inexplicably not invited to either the NCAA or the National Invitation Tournament. However, based largely on these two successful seasons, Yoder was offered and accepted the head men's coaching position at the University of Wisconsin-Madison. The UW position was then not a particularly attractive one, but as one commentator pointed out, "It's still the Big 10 and you get to live in Madison."

Cardinal assistant coach Al Brown was appointed men's head coach shortly after Yoder left. He inherited McCallum for his banner senior year with the main rebounding chores falling to transfer Jon Mansbury. The Cardinals had a solid year which featured an emotional victory in Muncie over Yoder's first Wisconsin team and a holiday tourney championship win over Karl Malone-led Louisiana Tech. But the Cardinals lost in the MAC tourney to Bowling Green and finished the year 17–12 and 10–8 in the MAC.

During the next year Brown pulled off a recruiting coup when he convinced former Indiana High School Mr. Basketball Dan Palombizio to transfer to Ball State after the 6' 8" forward decided to leave Purdue. Palombizio's powerful game was the key to Cardinal success during the 1985-86 season in which Ball State won the MAC tourney and continued on to the NCAA Tournament where they lost a first round contest to Memphis State, 95–63. The following year, with Palombizio gone, the Cards fell back in the pack once again finishing 9–18 for the season and 4–12 in the MAC. Two winning seasons out of five and a perceived lack of discipline, especially in some of his players' academic work, were enough to convince BSU administrators that a change in direction in the men's basketball program was necessary. Brown's contract was not renewed for the 1987-88 season.

Jim Holstein became the Cardinals head coach in 1972. An Ohio native, Holstein was a star athlete in basketball, football, and baseball at the University of Cincinnati. He also played professional basketball for the Minneapolis Lakers and the Fort Wayne Pistons. During his tenure as the Cardinals' head mentor, he compiled an overall 55-70 won-lost record and was 12–20 in the Mid-American Conference. He resigned from his position on February 9, 1977, effective at the conclusion of that season.

An Indiana All-Star and All-America selection as a high school senior, Larry Bullington was one of Ball State's prize recruits of the early 1970s. A long-range jump shooter of great skill, he set several Cardinal scoring records between 1971 and 1974. His records included 1,747 total points and a 23.6 points-per-game average. His one-game record of 47 points against Cleveland State on January 19, 1974, stood until January 5, 2003, when it was broken by Chris Williams' 48 points versus Akron. As a senior Bullington was the nation's sixth leading scorer (25.5 pts.), was selected team MVP, and named All-America Honorable Mention. In recent years, he has been a very successful men's basketball coach at Indianapolis Pike High School. Bullington was inducted into the BSU Athletics Hall of Fame in 1984.

Chris Collins goes up for a jump shot from the side. A fine scorer and perimeter player, Collins was one of the Cardinals "Muncie connection" recruits of the early 1970s.

Kim Kaufman, a local Muncie high school star, went to Rice University and transferred to Ball State for his last two years of eligibility in 1973–75. He was a gifted outside shooter with a soft touch whose long jumpers were crowd pleasers.

Shafer Suggs drives to the iron against Illinois State. Although mostly remembered for his outstanding football career which culminated with success in the NFL, Suggs also played basketball for the Cards for three seasons in the early-1970s. A spectacular rebounder, shot blocker, and dunker, he was a crowd favorite. He became a member of the BSU Athletics Hall of Fame in 1987.

Larry Heinbaugh battles for a rebound. A 6'-8" forward-center from Ohio, Heinbaugh was one of Ohio native Jim Holstein's Buckeye state recruits. An excellent student, Heinbaugh played a key inside role for the mid-1970s Cardinals.

(*left*) Coach Jim Holstein's staff in 1973 is pictured here, from left to right—Tom Dobbs, Holstein, and Carl Meditch.

Steve Moniaci (*below*), a graduate of Ball State's Honors College, was a student manager from 1975 to 1979. In recent years, he has been on the Athletics staff at Rice University where he currently serves as Senior Associate Athletic Director.

(*left*) Over the years the Ball State men's basketball program has been involved with a number of team schedule promotion campaigns. This picture-schedule card from 1973–1974, sponsored by a soft drink company, features a "collectible" shot of Cardinal backcourt star Bob Faulkner.

The 1974-75 junior varsity was coached by Cardinal legend Larry Bullington one year after he completed his eligibility. This team had seven freshmen and three sophomores during a season when four highly recruited first-year players were on the varsity roster. Number 30 in the first row is Matt Beerbower, who went on to letter for the varsity in his next three seasons. Ball State ended junior varsity competition one year later.

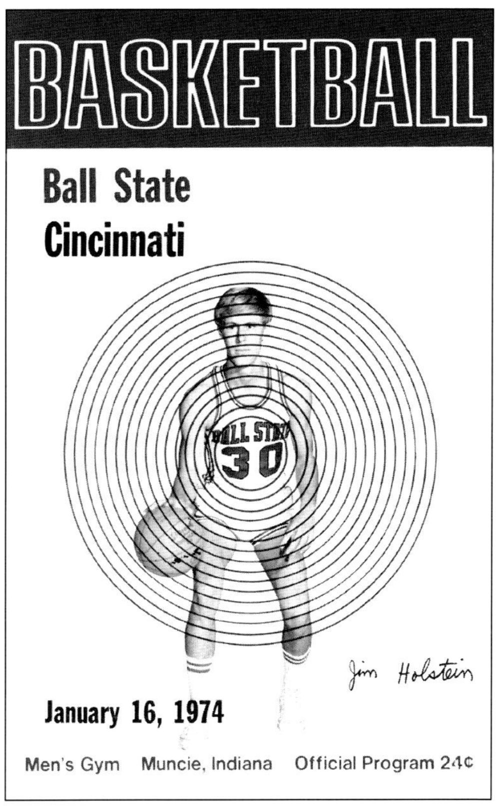

This Ball State-Cincinnati game program is a wonderful piece of Cardinal hoops family memorabilia. The featured player is Jim Holstein, the son of the Cardinals' head coach. The senior Holstein was a star for Cincinnati in the early 1950s. More importantly, the Cardinals upset the favored Bearcats, 99–82. Cincinnati never played in Muncie again!

A native of Plymouth, Indiana, Steve Yoder joined Jim Holstein as an assistant coach in 1976. He had previously held the same position at Furman. Named head coach in 1977, Yoder led the Cardinals to their first NCAA Division I Tournament appearance in 1981. He was selected as MAC Coach of the Year in both 1981 and 1982; his 1981 squad won the MAC Tournament, and the 1982 team captured the university's first outright MAC championship. His career record was 77–62 and 44–36 in the MAC. He was inducted into the BSU Athletics Hall of Fame in 2001.

Mike Drews goes up for a jump shot against Kent State. One of Coach Steve Yoder's best recruits, Drews led the Cardinals in scoring in his first two years (1977–79). He combined an accurate jump shot with aggressive moves to the hoop. He was forced to give up his last two seasons due to a heart problem but remained with the team as a student coach.

Randy Boarden tosses in a short jumper. From 1975–79, Boarden was the Cardinals best low post player. He combined smooth offensive moves with fine shot blocking and rebounding ability. Boarden still ranks in the top twenty of all-time BSU scorers with 1,290 points and is second in career rebounding (1,000) and blocked shots (131). He was an All-MAC second team selection in 1979.

Jim Hahn passes to a teammate. The Cardinals all-time career assist leader with 573, Hahn played from 1975–79. He was a highly-skilled passer, especially to BSU's post players and on the fast break. He was selected Academic All-America (6th team) in 1979 and was inducted into the BSU Athletics Hall of Fame in 1972.

George Bradley shoots over the Butler defense. A smooth forward-center for Coach Steve Yoder, Bradley was a dominant force on both ends of the court. He combined rebounding ability with an assortment of low-post moves.

Jim Fields attempts to turn the corner and drive the baseline. An accurate jump shooter and able passer, Fields was a BSU floor leader in the late 1970s.

Coach Steve Yoder's staff in 1979 consisted of, from left to right, Al Brown, Brad McNulty, and Yoder (kneeling).

Robert Sims (50) and the Cardinals in action against in-state rival Indiana State in the late 1970s. Number 33 for the visiting Sycamores is future NBA legend Larry Bird.

Al Gooden drives the lane. A skilled inside player of the late 1970s to early 1980s, Gooden was selected to the All-MAC second team on two occasions (1980 and 1981) and still shares the BSU record for best field goal percentage in a season, hitting 60 percent of his shots in 1979–80 and 58 percent from 1979 to 1981. He was named to the Ball State Athletics Hall of Fame in 1991.

Robert Sims was the team's MVP in 1977–78. A transfer from West Virginia, the 6' 8" Sims was an inside force in rebounding and scoring during his two years with the Cardinals.

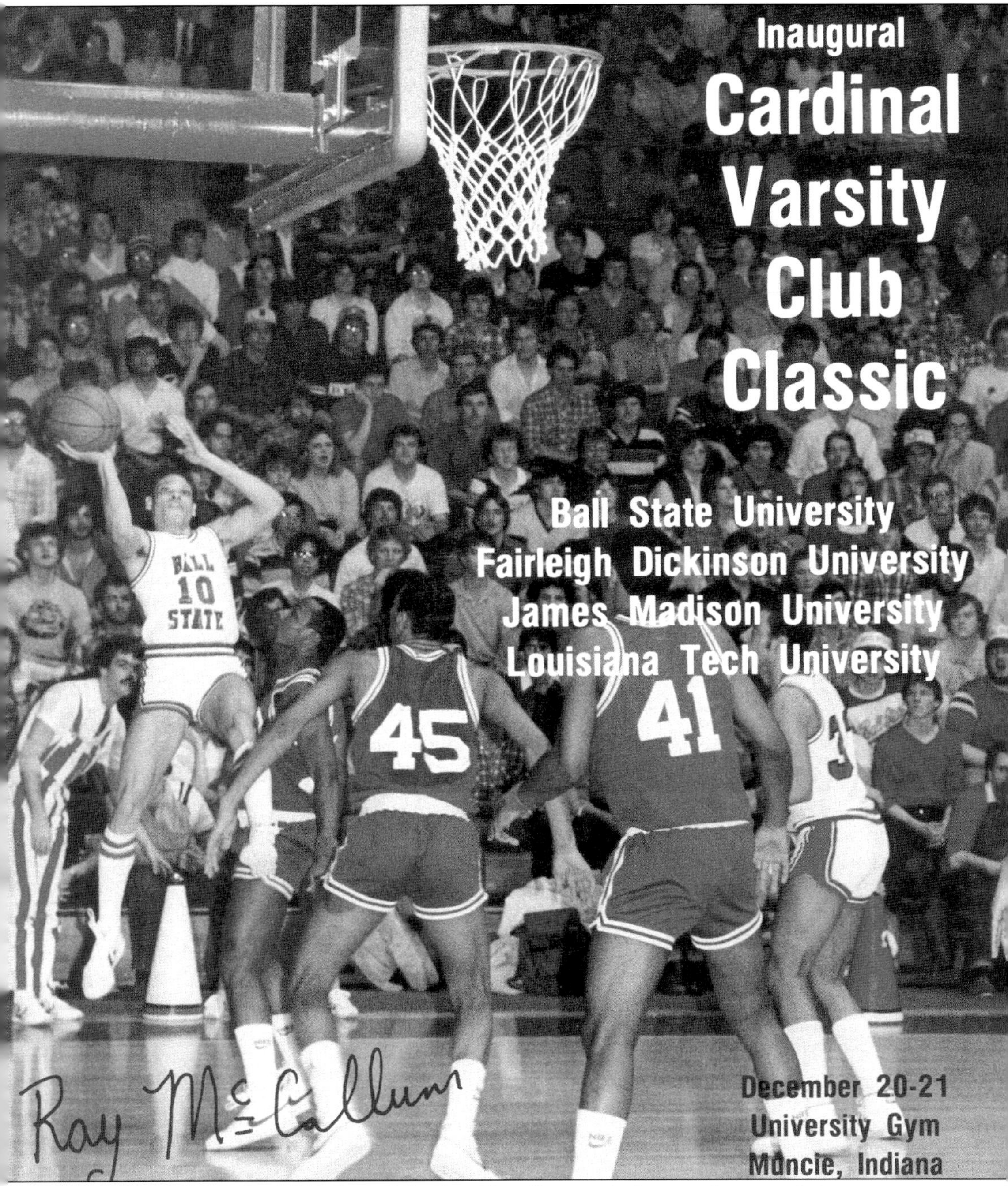

Ray McCallum lofts one over three defenders. An all around player with a superb long range jump shot, McCallum led the Cardinals to their first MAC championships in 1981 and 1982 and to the MAC tournament title and first NCAA appearance in 1981. By the time of his graduation he was the MAC's leading career scorer and had earned numerous all-MAC honors. In his senior year, he won the Naismith Award as the nation's outstanding senior under six feet tall. He is also the only Ball State University athlete to have his number (10) retired in any sport. McCallum was a 1993 inductee to the Cardinals' Athletics Hall of Fame.

John Williams shoots over a Toledo defender. A fine all-around player at both ends of the court, Williams was the Cardinals "Mr. Dependable" from 1978–82. He combined solid scoring ability with excellent passing skills and finished his career as one of BSU's career assist leaders (344). He was a 1992 inductee to the BSU Athletics Hall of Fame.

Jeff Williams at the pay-off end of a fast break. An Indiana All-Star from Logansport High School, Williams was an outside scorer for the Cardinals in the late 1970s and early 1980s. He was particularly effective coming off the bench.

C.C. Fullove battles for a rebound in the Cardinals' December 1980 victory over Nebraska. Fullove was a key player for Steve Yoder from 1980 to 1982. He had a high point game of 38 against Central Michigan in 1982, a contest in which he set a Cardinal record with 28 points in one half. He also is among Ball State's leaders for single season field goal percentage, shooting 57 percent in 1980–81, and he was selected team Most Valuable Player in 1982.

Ray McCallum goes down the baseline against Nebraska. Guarding McCallum is Nebraska star Jack Moore who, like McCallum, was a high school legend at Muncie Central High School. This game before a sold out University Gym crowd was a "homecoming" for Moore and the only time the two star guards ever played against each other in a regularly scheduled college game.

Ball State's 1980-81 MAC tourney champions and the first team to be selected to play in the NCAA Division I Tournament. From left to right are: (first row) Al Gooden, Jeff Williams, George Bradley, Clement Murrell, Mark Thurston, and John Williams; (second row) Ray McCallum, Rick Hampton, Jeff Parker, Student Coach Mike Drews, Bob Albertson, C.C. Fullove, and Jeff Furlin; (third row) Head Coach Steve Yoder, Assistant Coach Al Brown, Assistant Coach Brad McNulty, Student Managers Al Scott and Tom Brokaw, and Head Trainer Don Vogelgesang.

A display of trophy hardware for Ball State's first MAC championship in 1980–81.

Al Brown, a veteran Indiana high school coach, Purdue basketball staff member, and assistant to Steve Yoder, was named Cardinal men's head coach in 1982 following Yoder's departure for Wisconsin. From 1982 to 1987, he compiled a 68-75 overall won-lost record and 38-50 in the MAC. His 1986 Cardinals won the MAC Tournament and advanced to the NCAA Tournament, where they lost in the first round.

Coach Al Brown's staff in 1985 was, from left to right, Leonard Drake, Bill Hahn, and Al Brown.

Jon Mansbury shoots over the Miami defense. A 6' 7" forward from Indianapolis, Mansbury transferred to BSU from Texas Christian. In his two years with the Cardinals (1981–1983) he was a team leader in rebounding and an effective scorer from his forward position.

Rick Rowray goes to the iron. A Muncie Central star and Indiana University transfer, Rowray was a Cardinal leader from 1983 to 1985 until his career was ended by an elbow injury. During the 1983-84 season, he was team co-captain and led the squad in assists and steals. In 1985–86, he was a student coach.

Jeff Furlin attempts to drive around an Indiana University defender. A co-winner of the team MVP award in 1983–84, he was the first BSU player to be named to the MAC All-Academic first team.

Marcus Lacey with a baseline move. A 6' 7" center with rebounding and inside scoring skills, Lacey shared the Cardinals MVP award in 1983–84.

Chris Shelton lays one off the glass. From 1983 to 1986, Shelton was one of the Cards most well-rounded players, equally adept at scoring and passing. His 1,164 career points and 481 assists are still among Ball State's best.

Larry Reed drives the lane. An outstanding high school player in Milwaukee, Reed transferred to Ball State from South Plains Junior College in Texas and became one of the Cardinals leading guards and backcourt scorers from 1984 to 1986.

(*right*) Charles Smith rejects one. The Cardinals' "Elevator Man," Smith thrilled fans with his amazing shot-blocking ability during his career in the mid-1980s. Standing 6' 4", Smith had incredible timing and recorded a then record 86 rejections in 1986–87. He was an All-MAC second team selection in 1987 and scored 571 points in 1986–87.

(*below*) Men's basketball has always offered students the opportunity to try out for the team. Each year a few who participate in these basketball "cattle calls" make the squad. They receive no scholarship assistance but work hard in practice, usually on scout teams, and are sometimes "rewarded" with a spot on the roster for a road game. From time to time, a walk-on will impress the coaches enough that he will be offered a grant-in-aid, making all those hours of toil and sweat worthwhile. Here walk-on David Eha passes off. Eha was first awarded a grant-in-aid in his junior year (1985–86) after playing two seasons and impressing Coach Al Brown and his staff with his hustle and teamwork.

(*right*) Mike Chesser grabs one off the boards against Indiana University. A solid forward for the Cardinals of the mid-1980s, he was known for his rebounding ability and rugged defense.

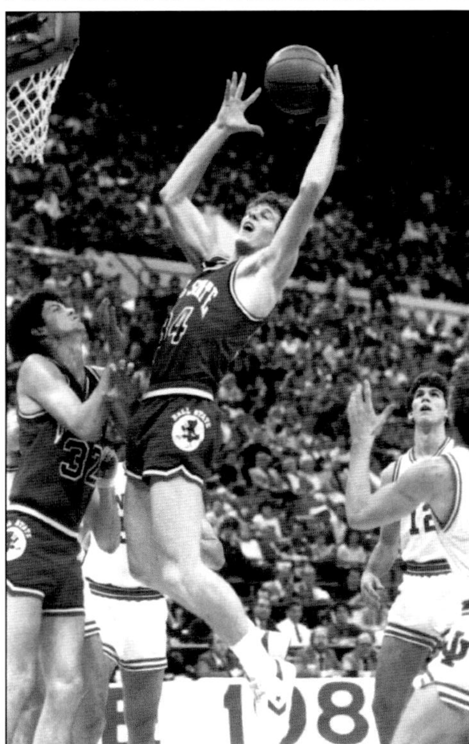

Dan Palombizio, former Mr. Indiana High School Basketball, shoots from the baseline against rival Indiana State. The highly recruited Palombizio spent 1982–83 at Purdue but became dissatisfied with his limited role there; he transferred to Ball State in 1984. As a Cardinal, he showed outstanding individual skills. In 1984–85, he ranked 3rd in the nation in scoring and 12th in rebounding. In 1985–86, he was selected as *Sports Illustrated* Player of the Week for March 3–9, and he led the Cardinals to victory in the MAC Tournament and a birth in the NCAA Tournament. He also holds the Ball State record for most points in a single season (762) and in two seasons (1,369). He was taken in the 7th round of the NBA draft by the Philadelphia 76ers.

Ball State's 1985-86 team that went 21–10, won the MAC tourney and lost in the NCAA tournament first round to Memphis State, 95–63. From left to right are: (first row) David Eha, Student Managers Steve Patterson and Brian West, Trainer Tony Cox, Head Coach Al Brown, Associate Coach Bill Hahn, Assistant Coach Leonard Drake, Graduate Assistant Steve Peters, and Charles Smith; (second row) Derrick Wesley, Rob Kamiak, Marx Clark, Dan Palombizio, John Whittington, Steve Dziatczak, Jeff Foresman, Rick Hall, Jon Luedke, Rick Rowray, Ron Peters, Larry Reed, and Chris Shelton.

Rick Majerus directs the Cardinals offense. When Majerus left his assistant coaching position with the NBA Milwaukee Bucks to become Ball State University's 13th head men's basketball coach in May 1987, the late Al McGuire said, "You have just hired the finest basketball mind in the country." By the time he left the Cardinals two years later to accept the head coaching position at the University of Utah, few Ball State University fans would disagree with McGuire's statement.

Six

NCAA Dreams and Nightmares

Rick Majerus and Dick Hunsaker

1987–1993

Ball State began a national search to find Al Brown's successor immediately after his departure. The usual number of Division I assistant coaches, anxious to move up, applied, but as Athletic Director Don Purvis sifted through the resumés of interested candidates, he discovered one quite unusual applicant, Milwaukee Bucks Assistant Coach and former Marquette head mentor, Rick Majerus. Tired of the grueling pace of the NBA schedule and recently married, Majerus was looking for a coaching position at a school in the Midwest that was a campus community. Cardinal administrators and fans were more than a little surprised that a coach with his credentials would be interested in the BSU position. Following a campus visit and interviews, the Wisconsin native was named head men's coach. He quickly assembled a staff, which most notably for the future of Cardinal basketball over the next several years, included Weber State assistant Dick Hunsaker.

Majerus was an entirely different style of coach, on and off the court, for Ball State. A personable, well-read, humorous, profane man in public and private conversation, he was a delight for the local media with his open, candid style. His coaching philosophy truly reflected his own blue collar background. He believed in controlling the tempo of the game (his practices were amazingly structured); emphasized team before self; and insisted on rugged "in-your-face" defense. He was also a zealous recruiter who, along with Hunsaker, knew where to find Division I players. The best example of this occurred shortly after Majerus arrived in Muncie when he convinced Ball State senior administrators to admit two players who had run into some legal difficulties involving the theft of a credit card at the University of Arkansas at Little Rock. Curtis Kidd and Paris McCurdy enrolled for fall 1987 and would be instrumental in reshaping Cardinal basketball one year later.

For the 1987-88 season, Majerus inherited Brown's players, whom he tried to mold to his style of basketball. It was a year of constant struggle. The fact that he led this team to a .500 record in both the season and the conference, 14–14 and 8–8, has lead many to view this accomplishment as Majerus's best coaching performance at any university.

But one year later, 1988–89, it was widely known throughout the Midwest at least that the Cardinals were loaded. This team performed beyond anyone's expectations. Led by Kidd and McCurdy, Ball State had its best season in history, 29–3 overall and 14–2 in the MAC, was nationally ranked in the polls, won the MAC tourney, and defeated Pitt in the first round of the NCAA tourney in Indianapolis before losing to Illinois. Along the way they knocked off three Big Ten opponents—Minnesota, Northwestern, and Purdue—a first in BSU annals. However, shortly after the completion of this dream season, Majerus decided to move to greener pastures and accepted the head job at the University of Utah.

Wasting little time to name his successor, the university promoted Majerus's top assistant, Dick Hunsaker, to the head coaching post. Hunsaker shared Majerus's coaching philosophy. He also had the same work ethic and the ability to find quality players, especially in the junior college and transfer ranks. But he lacked Majerus's outgoing personality, especially in dealing with fans and the media, which would eventually contribute to his undoing.

In 1989–90, the Cardinal cupboard was well-stocked. Kidd and McCurdy were now senior veterans, the rest of the team consisted of talented players who knew their roles well, and star recruit Chandler Thompson added a new offensive dimension. Few fans were surprised that the team went 26–7 and won the MAC regular season and tourney. What was shocking was their post-season NCAA tourney success, defeating Oregon State and Louisville to make the Sweet Sixteen where they lost a true heartbreaker to eventual national champion UNLV by two points.

These two back-to-back seasons of MAC and NCAA success brought a wave of unbridled euphoria to the Muncie campus. In a state where basketball is king but success is usually associated with universities in Bloomington and West Lafayette, this was a new feeling of pride for members of the Cardinal community—and they gloried in it!

Over the next three years, the Cardinals continued their winning ways, going to post-season tournaments each year. Led by a star-studded cast of talented players, Ball State was the class of the MAC and one of the best teams in the Midwest. In 1990–91, they lost to Cincinnati in the NIT. One year later they were sent out to Salt Lake City to face Majerus's Utah team in a NIT first round contest and once again lost, 72–57. However, the undoubted highlight of this season was the opening in January 1992, of the new University Arena, a spacious state-of-the-art facility seating 11,500. In 1992–93, the Cards were 26–8, tied for first in the MAC, and won the post-season tourney which got them a NCAA invitation. They headed north to Chicago where they were defeated, 94–72, by Kansas.

Over the next several months, Cardinal basketball fortunes took a decidedly negative turn. Simply stated, the NCAA Committee on Infractions found the men's basketball program guilty of several major rule violations involving recruiting and extra-benefits for players, while the university was cited for a "lack of institutional control." The penalties included the loss of one men's basketball scholarship for the 1994 to 1996 seasons.

On October 3, 1993, Dick Hunsaker resigned as men's head coach. An era of achievement and prominence in national men's basketball circles came to an ignominious end.

Derrick Wesley lays one in against Northern Illinois. Recruited by Coach Al Brown, Wesley completed his career as the leading scorer for first-year Coach Rick Majerus, which was a difficult transition for the Cardinal forward. A shooter of great skill, in his career he had one 38 point game, earned All MAC honors, and was BSU MVP. He was inducted into the Ball State Athletics Hall of Fame in 1998.

In 1989, Rick Hall, a four-year letterman, was selected as the first male recipient of the Walter Byers Postgraduate Scholarship by the NCAA. The award was in recognition of Hall's exemplary academic performance as a student-athlete. He had a 3.944 grade point ratio with a double major in accounting and political science while enrolled in the Honors College. He was also named Academic All-America during his junior and senior year and was the Cardinals' captain in 1988–89, a season that saw the team win the MAC season and tournament championships and defeat Pittsburgh in the first round of the NCAA Tournament. Hall used his scholarship to attend Northwestern University Law School and is now a practicing attorney in Indianapolis. In 2000, he became a member of the BSU Athletics Hall of Fame.

Paris McCurdy with the ball (*above left*), and Curtis Kidd in the low post (*above right*)—McCurdy and Kidd were recruited by Majerus in 1988 and became the backbone of Ball State's nationally recognized teams in 1988–89 and 1989–90. Noted primarily for their defensive prowess and fiery style of play, they led the Cardinals to their first NCAA tournament victory in 1989 and to the NCAA Sweet Sixteen in 1990.

Greg Miller works his Purdue defender in the Cardinals historic defeat of the Boilermakers. Miller was an important player coming off the bench for the late 1980s championship teams. His jumpers from behind the 3-point arc were great crowd pleasers.

Roman Muller moves for position in the paint. The 7' 1" center transferred to Ball State from Marquette and was an excellent rebounder and shot blocker.

Jubilant BSU fans storm the University Gym floor following the Cardinals' victory over Purdue in December 1988. The win was especially memorable because the Boilermakers had trounced the Cards the previous year, 96–47, the greatest margin of defeat for a BSU men's basketball team up to that time.

Scott Nichols starts up court against Pitt in BSU's first NCAA tourney victory. Nichols was the point guard on the championship teams of the Majerus-Hunsaker era. A fierce defender, "Nick" often drew the assignment of guarding the opposition's leading scorer. An excellent passer as well, he finished his playing days ranked fourth on the all-time career assist list (406).

Two outstanding players of Ball State's NCAA teams of the late 1980s, Greg Miller and Shawn Parrish, here visit a young patient at a local hospital. Ball State men's basketball has a proud tradition of its players doing volunteer work in the Muncie community.

Billy Butts starts the fast break. A transfer from the University of Michigan, Butts quickly became a leading perimeter scorer for the successful Majerus-Hunsaker NCAA Tournament teams. Twice selected MAC Tournament MVP (1989 and 1990), he was one of the Cardinals finest pure 3-point shooters.

A zealous 1989 Cardinal fan at a game against Miami—his t-shirt refers, of course, to then Indiana University Coach Bob Knight.

The 1988-89 Cardinals posted the best men's basketball won-lost mark, 29–3, in BSU history. From left to right are: (front row) Mike Spicer, Rodney Haynes, Mike Giunta, Keith Stalling, Rick Hall, Shawn Parrish, Scott Nichols, Dave Barber, and Billy Butts; (back row) Tutorial Coordinator Bruce Bohlander, Trainer Tony Cox, Associate Head Coach Dick Hunsaker, Head Coach Rick Majerus, Paris McCurdy, Tom Ahaus, Roman Muller, Curtis Kidd, Greg Miller, Associate Coach Leonard Drake, Graduate Assistant Tim Hopfensperger, Volunteer Assistant Kirk Earlywine, and Student Manager Tim Tummers.

Dick Hunsaker and Chandler Thompson celebrate Ball State's NCAA victory over Louisville. Hunsaker joined Rick Majerus's coaching staff during the summer of 1987 and quickly distinguished himself as an excellent recruiter. He became the Cardinals' head mentor in spring1989 when Majerus left for Utah. Several of his players received All-MAC honors, and his teams were known for their disciplined offense and tough defense. Following his resignation, Hunsaker held several coaching positions including four years as an assistant to Majerus at Utah. He is currently the head men's coach at Utah Valley State College.

Dick Hunsaker's staff in 1989–90 was, from left to right, Hunsaker, Vince Bertram, Leonard Drake, Ron Hecklinski, and Larry Eustachy.

Hunsaker's 1989-90 team played several games in the Netherlands and Belgium in August 1989 as part of a pre-season European tour, a time that many observers feel helped this special team bond as a unit. In this photograph, Paris McCurdy (left) and Mike Spicer pose after touring a wooden shoe factory.

Mike Spicer drives for two. A key player on Ball State's outstanding teams of the late 1980s and early 1990s, Spicer was a fierce defender and a skilled passer. He holds the school record for career games played (126).

"The Most Famous Basket in Ball State University History." Paris McCurdy's basket as the clock ran down tied the Cardinals with Gary Payton-led Oregon State in the first round of the NCAA Tournament in Salt Lake City, on March 15, 1990. McCurdy was fouled on the shot, made the free throw, and the Cardinals advanced to the second round where they defeated Louisville, 62–60. The following week, Ball State lost to eventual national champion UNLV, 69–67.

Pandemonium reigns in The Village, a shopping area adjacent to the Ball State campus, following the Cardinals upset victory over Louisville in the NCAA Tournament regional final in March 1990. (Courtesy of TIS Bookstore.)

Chandler Thompson skies for a dunk over Oregon State. An electrifying leaper, Thompson thrilled Ball State fans in the late 1980s and early 1990s with his wide assortment of inside moves, thundering dunks, and rebounding skills. He was the team's leading scorer on its run to the Sweet Sixteen. During his career he received All-MAC and national recognition on several occasions. For the past several years he has played in European professional leagues.

Keith Stalling lays in a deuce. A prep star from Chicago, Stalling was an outstanding scorer and tough defender for the late 1980s and early 1990s Cardinals' tournament teams. He was an All-Conference first-team selection in 1993.

Shawn Parrish puts one up off the glass. One of the few players to transfer to Ball State from the successful junior college program at Vincennes University, Parrish was a mainstay for the Cardinals' championship teams in 1989 and 1990. He combined excellent court savvy with an accurate jump shot and good inside moves along with what one opposition coach called "a nose for the ball." To Ball State fans of that era, he was just "Mr. Hustle."

Emanuel Cross drives to the hoop. A zealous defender with an effective long-range jump shot, Cross transferred to Ball State from the junior college ranks and quickly became a key player on the Cardinals' tournament teams of the late 1980s to early 1990s. He was named All-MAC First Team in 1991. Cross is Ball State's career leader in three-point field goal percentage with 46 percent from 1989 to 1991.

The opening game in University Arena. The Cardinals moved from the friendly confines of Irving Gymnasium to spacious University Arena, seating capacity 11,500, on January 15, 1992. In the inaugural game, they defeated archrival Miami University, 70–64. Since that date, the Arena, renamed to honor the 16-year presidency of Dr. John E. Worthen, who retired in July 2000, has been "friendly" as well—the Cardinals have won over 80 percent of their games played here. The facility houses the team's locker room, training, weight, and media rooms as well as lounges and coaches offices. It is also used for winter and summer commencement ceremonies and as a venue for guest lecturers and entertainers.

The Ball State Pep Band inspires the crowd during the opening game in University Arena.

(*left*) Bill Gillis jams one home. MAC Tournament MVP in 1992, Gillis was an inside force for the Cardinals in the early 1990s and one of the MAC's leading rebounders.

(*below*) David Broz puts in a reverse dunk. A fine student-athlete, Broz was a solid low-post player in the early 1990s.

(*left*) Cardinals' guard Jeff Robbins with United States Senator Richard Lugar of Indiana during a 1992 Summer Internship in Washington. A Muncie high school star, Robbins transferred to Ball State after playing for two years at Murray State. He was a key BSU reserve from 1990 to 1992.

(*right*) Jamie Matthews heads up court on a fast break. One of the Cardinals' premier point guards on the successful teams of the early 1990s, Mathews had excellent court vision along with a consistent perimeter jump shot and accuracy from the free throw line. He was named to the MAC All-Tournament team in 1993 and holds the school record for most assists in a season (207).

(*below*) Jeermal Sylvester hits from the side. From 1990–94, Sylvester was one of the Cardinals' leading scorers and rebounders. A multi-talented player, he is among the school's leaders in career scoring (1,410 points) and rebounds (529).

(*right*) Walk-on Matt Winders defends the low post against Ohio University. Winders earned three letters for the Cardinals from 1991 to 1994 and played in several games, including Ball State's first-round NCAA tourney contest with Kansas.

The best NCAA tourney team in Ball State history, the 1989-90 Cardinals were, from left to right: (front row) Billy Butts, Mike Giunta, Scott Nichols, and Mike Spicer; (middle row) David Barber, Rodney Haynes, Shawn Parrish, Curtis Kidd, Keith Stalling, Greg Miller, and Paris McCurdy; (back row) Academic Advisor Mike Mahan, Tutorial Coordinator Bruce Bohlander, Student Manager Tim Tummers, Chandler Thompson, Emanuel Cross, Assistant Coach Ron Hecklinski, Associate Coach Leonard Drake, Mark Hardwick, Volunteer Coach Vince Bertram, Assistant Coach Larry Eustachy, Trainer Tony Cox, and Head Coach Dick Hunsaker.

The 1990-91 Cardinals finished 21–10 and lost to Cincinnati in the National Invitation Tournament, BSU's first appearance in this post-season event. From left to right are: (front row) Mark Hardwick, Matt Winders, Keith Stalling, Rodney Holmes, Emanuel Cross, Chandler Thompson, Mike Spicer, Jeermal Sylvester, Todd Jones, and Jeff Robbins; (back row) Trainer Tony Cox, Tutorial Coordinator Bruce Bohlander, Academic Advisor Mike Mahan, Associate Coach Leonard Drake, David Broz, Bill Gillis, Steve Turner, Marcus Johnson, Strength Coordinator Wade Russell, Assistant Coach Ron Hecklinski, Volunteer Coach Vince Bertram, and Head Coach Dick Hunsaker.

Ball State's 1991-92 team finished 24–9 and went to the National Invitation Tournament where they lost to Utah 72–57. From left to right are: (front row) Jeff Robbins, Rodney Holmes, Mark Hardwick, Mike Spicer, Keith Stalling, Jamie Matthews, and Chandler Thompson; (back row) Associate Coach Leonard Drake, Head Coach Dick Hunsaker, Associate Coach Ron Hecklinski, Jeermal Sylvester, David Broz, Steve Turner, Bill Gillis, William Berry, Matt Winders, Assistant Coach Glenn Hefferman, Equipment Manager Dave Plum, and Trainer Tony Cox.

Coach Dick Hunsaker greets Rick Majerus before the Cardinals NIT loss to Utah in Salt Lake City. The person to Hunsaker's left is former Ball State assistant Kirk Earlywine, who was then on Majerus's Utah staff.

Ball State's 1992-93 team tied for first in the MAC, won the MAC tourney, and advanced to the NCAA Tournament where they lost to Kansas, 94–72, in a first round game. From left to right are: (front row) Jamie Matthews, Rodney Holmes, Quentin Benson, Matt Winders, David Hall, Jeremy Crittendon, Jeermal Sylvester, Markee James, and Mark Hardwick; (back row) Head Coach Dick Hunsaker, Associate Coach Leonard Drake, Greg Miller, Steve Turner, Bill Gillis, David Broz, Steve Payne, Associate Coach Ron Hecklinski, Eric Foister, and Trainer Tony Cox.

Seven

A Rescue Mission and the Return of a Former Assistant Coach

Ray McCallum and Tim Buckley

1993–2003

As the opening of practice for the 1993-94 season approached, the Cardinals busily searched for a new coach. Two candidates came to campus for interviews, Purdue assistant Bruce Weber and Michigan assistant and former Ball State star Ray McCallum. It was no surprise to Cardinal fans that McCallum got the call to try to bring the troubled program back to MAC and NCAA respectability. For the first time in Ball State history, the university's athletic programs were on NCAA probation for two years as a result of recruiting and extra benefits violations involving men's basketball.

After graduating from BSU, McCallum joined Steve Yoder's Wisconsin staff and earned a reputation as an outstanding recruiter. He had joined the Wolverines only a few months before the BSU position became available. With a Ball State staff made up of Hunsaker's assistants, McCallum began the task of introducing a veteran Cardinal team to his style of play at both ends of court.

With All-MAC Steve Payne, the team's dominant scorer and rebounder, McCallum's first team finished 16–12 overall and 11–7 in the MAC. By the following year, more familiar with McCallum's style of play and leadership, the Cardinals finished 21–11 and 11–7 in the conference but hit a hot streak in the MAC tourney and won it with a 77-70 victory over a fine Eastern Michigan team. They went on to the NCAA Tournament and lost to a talented Arizona State club, 81–66, in the first round.

The next year, 1995–96, was truly the beginning of a new era in BSU hoops history: the Time of Bonzi. Now a sophomore, Bonzi Wells, like his coach, was a super talent from local Muncie Central High School. An "all-everything" prep player, Wells was a franchise maker but also at times a temperamental individual on and off the court. Coaching the Cardinals was one challenge for McCallum; dealing with the often-undisciplined antics of Wells and a few other BSU players was an equally demanding one.

For three years, the Cardinals continued their winning ways. Wells was the team's leading scorer and rebounder in each of those seasons posting numbers that early on impressed professional scouts. However, as a team Ball State's often inconsistent play did not result in the now expected championships and post-season national tournament appearances until Wells's last year. In 1997–98, the Cardinals reached the twenty win mark for the first time since 1993 tied for first in the MAC West with a 14-4 mark; but lost a heartbreaker to Eastern Michigan in the MAC Tourney final, 93–92. Ball State accepted an NIT bid and was crushed by Memphis in the first round, 90–67. Wells completed his record-setting career winning honors from every quarter, including First-Team All-America in one publication. He was drafted by the Detroit Pistons as the 11th selection in the NBA draft, although they quickly traded him to the Portland Trail Blazers where he has been a team leader for several years.

In 1998–99 the Cardinals rebuilt, led by penetrating guard and perimeter scorer Duane Clemens, but their record fell to 16–11, 10–8 in the MAC, and they lost to arch-rival Miami in the MAC tourney.

The following year, the Cardinal offense was once again led by the slick Clemens, but rebounding leadership was taken over by a heralded freshman recruit from Florida, Theron Smith. With this outside-inside combination and a solid supporting cast, Ball State had McCallum's finest coaching year. They completed the season with a 22-9 record and 11–7 in the MAC for a first place conference tie and won the MAC tourney crown. Advancing on to the NCAA Tournament, they played an excellent first round game with nationally ranked UCLA before losing, 65–57.

In six years at the Cardinal helm, McCallum succeeded in guiding the basketball program's return to good standing with the NCAA, one major thing he was charged to do by BSU administrators, and it was no easy task. The team went through some great highs and lows under his leadership, on and off the court, but his critics were quick to see the program as one lacking discipline. Yet his record of wins and losses was on the plus side of the ledger, and this as much as anything else made him a good prospect to move to a more prestigious Division I position. Soon after the conclusion of the 1999-2000 season, McCallum announced that he was leaving Muncie to accept the head job at the University of Houston, a once national power that had fallen on hard times.

Ball State lost little time in searching for McCallum's successor and selected his former assistant, Tim Buckley, who had left BSU after the 1998-99 campaign to join Tom Crean's staff at Marquette. Buckley had been a head coach at Rockford (Illinois) College and a member of Stu Jackson's staff at UW-Madison. Highly skilled at game preparation and a fine recruiter, Buckley had also earned a reputation during his time as a Cardinal assistant as one who truly cared about his players' academic progress.

His first Cardinal team finished 18–12 and 11–7 in the MAC. However, in his second year, the team made national headlines in the pre-season and finished the year going deep into the NIT. Ball State journeyed to the Maui (Hawaii) Invitational in November 2001 expecting to provide warm-up competition for several national powers. In their first game, they faced #3 ranked Kansas, took them down to the wire and won, 93–91. The next day it was UCLA's turn, and the red-hot Cards destroyed the 4th ranked Bruins, 91–73. Twenty-four hours later, it was #1 ranked Duke in the tourney finals. The Cardinals played a hard-fought game before losing, 83–71. A second place finish in this nationally televised tourney brought the team a wave of acclaim not seen since the Majerus-Hunsaker years. Ball State was again in the national rankings until they lost December games to Indiana University and Butler. For the rest of the regular season, the Cards struggled but still managed to tie for first in the MAC West. They lost to Bowling Green in the MAC tourney but with a twenty-win season and their amazing Maui start, received an invitation to the NIT. As the other "bookend" to a season that had begun on such a high note, the Cards won three NIT games over South Florida, St. Joseph's, and LSU before losing at South Carolina, 82–47, in the Elite Eight.

The 2002-2003 season was one of great pre-season promise. The only down note was the fact that Theron Smith had spent much of the summer and fall rehabilitating a knee he had injured in a summer 2002 post-season NBA workout. But the team seemed destined for MAC and, fans hoped, post-season success. The backcourt was solid with shooters Chris Williams, and Matt McCollom, and Buckley's recruiting had added inside post-player Cameron Echols from the junior college ranks. In late November, the team traveled north to play in the Top of the World Classic in Fairbanks, Alaska. After the first game, it was obvious that Smith had not fully recovered from his injury. By the end of this tourney, the Cards future could almost be predicted.

Smith's knee needed more rehab, and he left the team to continue that process with a goal of returning in 2003–2004 for his last year. That left the Cardinals without their franchise player and forced Buckley to play two untested freshmen at the inside post positions with Echols. In addition, senior Rob Robbins, an outside scoring threat, suffered a career-ending knee injury in December 2002 and was forced to miss the rest of the season. It was to be a very long year! Although Williams had a record-setting senior season and Echols and the young inside players tried valiantly, the Cardinals suffered through their first losing season since 1986–87. After the season concluded, Smith announced that he would forgo his final year of eligibility and enter the NBA draft. His decision ended a period of Ball State having an outstanding "go to" player in the starting line-up, something that had begun with Bonzi Wells in the mid-1990s.

(*right*) Ray McCallum directs his players in the 2000 NCAA tournament. One of Ball State University's premier players, McCallum became the Cardinals 15th head coach in October 1993, after spending nine years as an assistant at Wisconsin and Michigan. In seven seasons, he guided the Cardinals to a 126-76 record, which included one 20-win season and three appearances in post-season tournament play. In many respects McCallum was a "town and gown" coach. He was involved in several community service endeavors and, of equal importance, required that his players participate in such off-campus activities as well.

(*below*) Mark Hardwick on the fast break. Recruited by Rick Majerus, Hardwick came to Ball State from nearby Jay County High School and became a valuable player under coaches Dick Hunsaker and Ray McCallum. He was one of the few players to play under three different BSU head mentors. He also participated in three post-season tournaments. Hardwick was a fan favorite for his long-range jump shot.

(*right*) Steve Payne dunks over two Bowling Green Falcons. A inside power player of the first rank, Payne dominated the paint for the Cardinals from 1992–95. An All-MAC selection in 1994 and 1995 and twice MAC Tournament MVP (1993 and 1995), he is among the team's all-time leaders in successful career free throws (342), rebounds (885), and total points scored (1,440).

(*left*) Randy Zachary releases a three-pointer. A fine perimeter scorer and passer as well as a hustling defender, Zachary was a backcourt "iron man" from 1993–1997. He ranks fifth on the BSU list for most minutes played in a career (3344) as well as second in most three-point field goals (161).

(*below*) Marcus Norris goes up for a jump shot. A transfer from Lansing (Michigan) Community College, Norris was a Cardinal scoring leader in the mid-1990s. His 65 three-pointers in 1994–95 still ranks with BSU's best.

(*left*) Mickey Hosier brings the ball up court. Hosier, from nearby Alexandria High School, led the Cardinals from the backcourt in the late 1990s. Always more interested in passing and defending, Hosier could shoot the three when he had to—often, it seemed, in response to the crowd's shouts of, "Shoot, Mickey, shoot."

(*right*) LaSalle Thompson attempts a 3-pointer. A transfer from Indiana State, Thompson was a skilled offensive performer of the mid-1990s. His 66 three-point field goals in 1995–96 rank him among the Cards all-time season leaders.

(*below*) Marcus Mason on the "D." Named team Most Valuable Player after his senior season (1998–99), Mason was a consistent rebounder and especially effective from beyond the 3-point arc.

(*right*) Shane Franks walked on at Ball State in 1998 after playing at Mercer University for two years on a basketball scholarship. He was a key reserve in his two seasons with the Cardinals and eventually earned a full grant-in-aid.

Currently one of the leading scorers for the NBA Portland Trail Blazers, Bonzi Wells came to Ball State from local Muncie Central High School where he was named All-State and an Indiana All-Star. From 1994–95 through 1997–98, he became the Cardinals' "go to" player with a soft jump shot, smooth post-up moves, and rebounding and defensive skills. Wells set numerous BSU and MAC records and was named All-MAC, MAC Player of the Year, and first team All-America (*Basketball Weekly*).

Bonzi Wells visits a local elementary school as part of a community service program.

Mickey Hosier participates in a junior reading program.

The 1994-95 Cardinals won the MAC Tournament and advanced to the NCAA tourney, where they lost to Arizona State in the first round. From left to right are: (front row) Bonzi Wells, Marcus Norris, LaSalle Thompson, Randy Zachary, Charles Smith, and DeWayne Rogers; (back row) Assistant Coach Butch McClintock, Assistant Coach Tracy Dildy, Steve Smith, Amos Gregory, Steve Payne, Ryan Reed, Head Coach Ray McCallum, and Assistant Coach Tim Buckley.

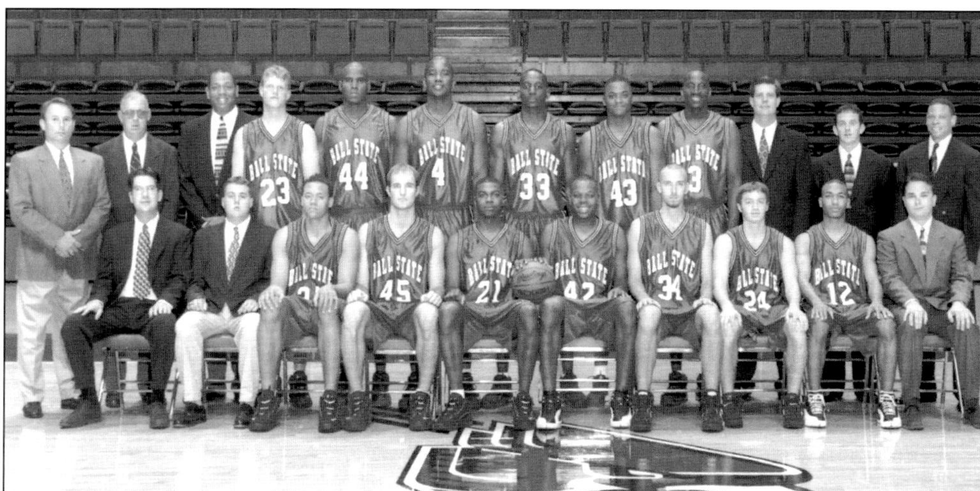

The 1997-98 Ball State team finished 21–8 and was selected to play in the National Invitation Tournament. They lost to Memphis in the first round, 90–67. From left to right are: (front row) Student Manager Jeremy Davies, Student Manager Andy Zickgraf, Mitch Hankins, Ryan Reed, Charles Smith, Bonzi Wells, Doug Clark, Mickey Hosier, Duane Clemens, and Student Manager Brett Eltzroth; (back row) Trainer Tony Cox, Equipment Manager Dave Plum, Assistant Coach Jerry Francis, Nick Wise, Jermaine Blackwell, Wayne Johnson, Marcus Mason, Lamont Roland, Jerome Davis, Assistant Coach Tim Buckley, Assistant Coach Artie Pepelea, and Head Coach Ray McCallum.

Duane Clemens pulls up for a jump shot. One of the few Muncie Southside Rebels to play for Ball State in recent years, Clemens was a crowd favorite throughout his career from 1996–2000. An outstanding penetrator from the two-guard slot, he also had a soft jumper from the arc and slashing moves to the basket on the fast break. He was a team leader in steals and ranks among Cardinal leaders in this career category. He is among the school's all-time leaders in total points scored (1,585) and career field goals (585).

The 1999-2000 Ball State team had a 22-9 record, won the MAC West Division title and the MAC tournament, and went to the NCAA tourney where they lost the UCLA, 65–57, in the first round. From left to right are: (front row) Student manager Nick Middleton, Mark Farris, Shane Franks, Rob Robbins, Patrick Jackson, Duane Clemens, Mickey Hosier, Cedric Moodie, Josh Murray, and Student Manager Steve Farmer; (back row) Head Coach Ray McCallum, Equipment Manager Dave Plum, Assistant Coach Scot Bunnell, Assistant Coach Jerry Francis, David Galley, Brian Burns, Lonnie Jones, Corey Harris, Theron Smith, Assistant Coach John Fitzpatrick, Student Manager Brendan Kirsch, Trainer Tony Cox, and Student Trainer Chester Coon.

Coach Tim Buckley in a reflective mood. The Cardinals' current head basketball coach, Buckley is on his "second time around" at Ball State. In May 2000, he became the Cardinal's 16th head men's basketball coach and brought to the position a solid coaching background at several levels of competition. An outstanding recruiter and strict disciplinarian, Buckley led Ball State to winning seasons in his first two campaigns including a run to the Elite Eight of the 2002 NIT.

Ball State's team is relaxed and ready at the November 2001 Maui Invitational. The Cardinals defeated nationally ranked Kansas and UCLA before losing in the tourney final to then #1 ranked Duke. (Courtesy of the EA SPORTS Maui Invitational and photographer Stewart Pinsky.)

Chris Williams drives for a lay-up against Duke in the Maui Invitational. (Courtesy of the EA SPORTS Maui Invitational and photographer Stewart Pinsky.)

Patrick (Petie) Jackson at the start of a Cardinal fast break. A fine passer, three-point scorer, and hard-working defender, Jackson was one of the Cardinals' best all-around point guards. By the end of his senior year (2001–2002), he was BSU's team leader in career three-point field goals with 202 from beyond the arc and a first-team Academic All-America.

Billy Lynch drives around an Indiana University defender. A two-sport player (football and basketball) for the Cardinals of the late 1990s to early 2000s, Lynch always joined the team late following the football season and provided immediate spark with his energetic, enthusiastic style of play.

Lonnie Jones sends one back. The big man as shot blocker personified, Jones struck fear into opponents who came near the iron throughout his Cardinal career from 1998–2002. With often uncanny timing, Jones rejected 301 shots, the BSU career record. He also blocked 89 in 2001–02 for the single season record.

Rob Robbins lets one go from "downtown." A fine long-range jump shooter, Robbins thrilled Cardinal fans with his ability to come off the bench and provide "instant offense."

Theron Smith goes to the hoop. Smith was an impact player since his freshman year (1999–2000). A prize high school recruit from Winter Haven, Florida, he earned several MAC honors as the Cardinals scoring and rebounding leader and was the 2002-2003 pre-season favorite to be the MAC's Player of the Year. In March 2003, he decided to forgo his last year of eligibility and enter the 2003 NBA draft, where he was not selected. Later, however, he signed a contract with the Memphis Grizzlies. Smith concluded his BSU career with 1,553 points to rank seventh on the Cards all-time list.

Chris Williams releases a jumper. An outstanding Chicago high school player, Williams transferred to Ball State from Loyola-Chicago in 2000. From 2001 to 2003, he was the Cardinals' leading backcourt scorer, combining an accurate long-range jump shot with twisting drives to the hoop. Williams had a record-setting year in 2002–2003, when he broke the one-game BSU scoring record with a 48 point total against Akron and finished the year with 736 total points to rank second on the Cardinals' all-time single season scoring list. He was named to the All-MAC first team and received the Phillips Award as BSU's Most Valuable Player.

Chris Ulm on a "Wear White to Support Your Team" game day. A senior during the 2002-2003 season, Ulm set a new standard for student managers. In addition to performing well the myriad tasks assigned to these students, he managed to turn such mundane chores as wiping water off the floor into a "moon walking" art form to the great delight of Cardinal fans, both home and away. At the Top of the World Classic in Alaska, he received the Outstanding Student Manager Award.

A raucous Cardinal student section cheers on the home team.

The 2001-2002 Ball State team that finished 23–12 overall and 12–6 for first place in the MAC West. They went to the National Invitation Tournament and made its Elite Eight. From left to right are: (first row) Mark Farris, Zach Willingham, Matt McCollom, Rob Robbins, Patrick Jackson, Billy Lynch, Chris Williams, Michael Bennett, and Gabe Miller; (second row) Head Coach Tim Buckley; Assistant Coach Scot Bunnell, Head Manager Chris Ulm, Student Trainer Blair Unruh, Robert Owens, Theron Smith, Lonnie Jones, Brian Burns, Scott Bushong, Head Manager Brady Days, Administrative Assistant Brent Bond, Athletic Trainer Tony Cox, Assistant Coach Tracy Webster, and Assistant Coach Angres Thorpe.

Service to Ball State's Men's Basketball

The Ball State men's basketball team has been richly blessed by having a long history of people, some quite visible, some more behind the scenes, who have made, and in some cases continue to make, significant contributions to the team. Pictured here are a representative few who are a part of this Cardinal community.

(*left*) Gayle Replogle at the scorer's table. A long-time Ball State academic advisor now retired, Replogle was the team's official scorer for 25 years, leaving this position at the conclusion of the 2002-03 season. During his quarter century of marking score sheets, he estimates that he recorded over 53,000 points!

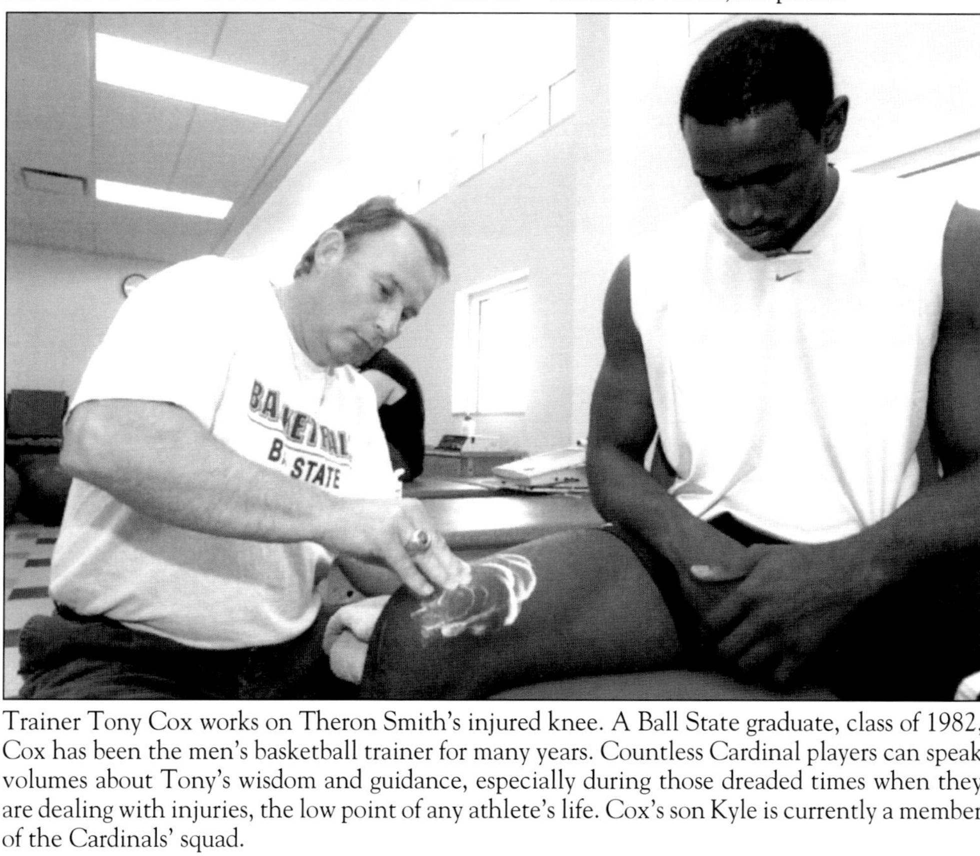

Trainer Tony Cox works on Theron Smith's injured knee. A Ball State graduate, class of 1982, Cox has been the men's basketball trainer for many years. Countless Cardinal players can speak volumes about Tony's wisdom and guidance, especially during those dreaded times when they are dealing with injuries, the low point of any athlete's life. Cox's son Kyle is currently a member of the Cardinals' squad.

Morry Mannies with former BSU players Shawn Parrish on the left and Dr Bob Faulkner on the right. The Voice of Cardinal basketball for nearly half a century, Mannies has shared the highs and lows of Ball State hoops. He has been inducted into both the Ball State Athletics Hall of Fame and the Indiana Basketball Hall of Fame, as well as having been named Indiana Sportscaster of the Year three times. Starting with the 2001-2002 season, he began the novel practice of using former Cardinal players as color commentators.

Jerry Peirson and Vince Welch prepare for game duty. Peirson, the former head men's coach at Miami University and currently BSU's Director of Athletics Development, and Welch, a Ball State graduate, handle the television coverage of Cardinals' men's Basketball.

Charlie Cardinal, here attempting to inspire the crowd in his "house" during a 2001 home game, has been the BSU Athletic Mascot since 1969.

EPILOGUE

Ball State's men's basketball team will prepare for the 2003-2004 season facing some significant challenges. Star forward Theron Smith's decision not to return to school and the graduation of super scorer Chris Williams have left significant holes in the Cardinals' program, ones that will have to be filled with players who are either new recruits or veterans who will have to take on new responsibilities.

In a broader context, the university is carefully examining its entire intercollegiate program because of a large deficit in the athletics budget. As people discuss these issues, some friends of Cardinals' sports have begun to worry that Ball State is moving too far in the direction of big time intercollegiate athletics and too far away from the original institutional commitment to "athletics for all." As others point out, however, historical trends suggest that a university like Ball State needs a strong intercollegiate program in major sports.

We believe that as the university carries on this conversation, men's basketball will continue to play a crucial role at Ball State. Although it has probably had more downs than ups in its eight decades, the successes of the past dozen years and, especially, Head Coach Tim Buckley's commitment to academic as well as athletic achievement, mean that Cardinal fans can look to the future with guarded optimism.

APPENDIX A

Letter Winners

Abbott, James (1945–46)
Ahaus, Tom (1989)
Albertson, Bob (1981–82)
Allison, Harry (1947–48–49)
Anderson, Rick (1968–69)
Anson, Harold (1932)
Arnett, Kim (1973–74–75–76)
Ashley, Ray (1939–40–41)
Baer, Charles* (1950)
Baker, Gary* (1974–75)
Baker, Phil (1970–71)
Baker, Roscoe (1920)
Banker, Jerry (1956)
Barber, Dave (1989–90)
Barker, Hubert (1929–30)
Barkman, Dick (1958)
Barnett, Steve (1971)
Barr, Foster (1935)
Beerbower, Matt (1976–77–78)
Beghun, Jerry (1964–65)
Belcher, Aaron (1920–23)
Bennett Michael (2002–03)
Benson, Quentin (1993)
Berry, William (1992)
Bettenhausen, Rick (1987–88)
Blair, Hubert (1922–23)
Blake, Floyd (1922–23)
Blankinship, Josh* (2001)
Blevins, Jim (1955)
Boarden, Randy (1976–77–78–79)
Bogacki, Jeff* (2002–03)
Bolander, Terrell (1935)
Bowman, Garr (1924–25)
Boyd, Bob (1971–72–73)
Boyd, Duane (1951–52)
Bradley, George (1978–79–80–81)
Bragg, Ted (1920)
Brokaw, Tom* (1980–81–82–83)
Brown, Edgar (1967)
Brown, Matt* (1994–95–96–97)
Brown, Pres (1955–56–57)
Broz, David (1991–92–93–94)
Brubaker, Harold (1919–23)
Bullington, Larry (1972–73–74)
Burlingame, Steve (1969)
Burns, Brian (1999–00–01–02)
Burnworth, Joe* (1960)
Bushong, Scott (2002)
Bussard, Ned (1940–41)
Butler, Ed (1962–63–64)
Butts, Billy (1989–90)
Caldwell, Shelby (1921)
Callan, Joe* (1962)
Campbell, Dean (1959)
Campbell, Herman* (1932)
Campbell, Larry (1952–53)
Canine, Jon (1971–72–73)
Carmichael, Carl (1922)
Carmichael, Jon (1982–83)
Carmichael, Robert (1946–48–49)
Carper, Robert (1976–77–79)
Carr, Wendell (1935)
Carroll, Dennis (1974)
Casterline, Donnie (1936–37–38)
Casterlow, John (1956)
Cates, Kevin (2003)
Caudill, Ike (1971–72)
Chalk, Dave* (1975–76)
Chesser, Mike (1982–83–84–85)
Christmon, Ken* (1983)
Clark, Bill (1972–73)
Clark, Doug (1998)
Clark, Marx (1983–84–85–86)
Clason, William (1939–40–41)
Clemens, Duane (1997–98–99–00)
Cly, Paul (1929–30–31–32)
Cole, Austin* (1932)
Collier, Paul (1929–30–31–32)
Collins, Chris (1972–73–74)
Connelley, Ralph (1922)
Conrads, Charles (1937)
Cook, Albert (1959)
Cottrell, Sam* (1997)
Cox, Jim* (1993)
Cox, Kyle (2003)
Craig, David (1925)
Crawford, Bob (1957–58)
Crittendon, Jeremy (1993)
Cross, Emanuel (1990–91)
Cross, Jack (1952–53–54–55)
Crowe, Bob (1960–61–62)
Cupp, David* (1997–98–99)
Daugherty, Wynn (1926)
Davis, Jerome (1998–99)
Davis, Stan (1953–54–55–60)
Davis, Wilbur, (1956–57–58–59)
Days, Brady* (2001–02–03)
Deaton, Mike (1994)
Delk, Ken (1952–53)
Denman, Jerry* (1979)
Dick, Dorwin (1930–31–32)
Dick, Marvin (1931–33)
Dickman, Ken* (1969)
Dobbs, Tom (1954–55–56–57)
Dotson, Dave* (1983–84–85)
Dotson, Don (1975)
Douglas, Charles (1975–76)
Doversberger, Richard* (1947)
Drews, Mike (1978–79/St. Coach 81)
Dunwiddie, Dave* (1961)
Durr, Ernest (1920)
Dziatczak, Steve (1985–86–87–88)
Ebrite, Ernest (1922–23)
Ebrite, Norman (1941–42–43)
Echols, Cameron (2003)
Edwards, Norm (1952–53–54)
Egger, John (1955–56)
Eha, David (1985–86–87–88)
Eltzroth, Brett* (1997–98)
England, Charles (1919)
Engle, Robert (1945)
Ervin, Curt (1964–65–66)
Etzler, Leland* (1960)
Evans, Joe (1942–43)
Farmer, Steve* (2000–01)
Farris, Mark (2000–01–03)
Faulkner, Bob (1973–74–75)
Faulkner, Doug (1984–85–86–87)
Feasel, Marion (1935)
Fields, Jim (1975–76–77–78)
Fields, Ron (1969)
Fisher, Jim (1980)
Fisher, Larry (1961)
Fleming, Marlon (1994)
Flint, Verne (1921)
Foresberg, Howard (1948–49–50)
Forsman, Andrew (2003)
Fortney, Harry* (1919)
Foust, Warren* (1992–93)
France, Todd* (1997)
Franks, Shane (1999–00)
Frederick, Randy (1969–70–71)
Fullhart, Ted (1957–58–59)
Fullove, C.C. (1981–82)
Fulmer, Moulton (1926–27–28–29)
Furlin, Jeff (1981–82–83–84)
Fyffe, Ron* (1968–69–70)
Galley, David (1999–00)
Galloway, Ron (1963–64)
Galt, Jim* (1983–84–85)
Garber, Ron (1950–51–52)
Gardner, Roy (1939–40)

Gegax, Gary (1972–73)
Gideon, Brad* (1992)
Gilbert, James (1994)
Gillis, Bill (1991–92–93)
Giunta, Mike (1988–90)
Goldman, Mel* (1962–64)
Gooden, Al (1979–80–81)
Goodwin, Gerald (1950–51–52)
Gordon, Marv*(1951–52–53)
Grabner, Loren* (1957)
Green, Hal* (1970–71)
Gregory, Amos (1995)
Griffith, George* (1964)
Grimes, Fred (1946–47)
Hahn, Jim (1976–77–78–79)
Hall, David (1992–93)
Hall, Rick (1986–87–88–89)
Hampton, Rick (1981–82)
Haney, John (1967)
Hankins, Mitch (1997–98)
Harbit, Ted (1955)
Harding, George (1919)
Hardwick, Mark (1991–92–93–94)
Harmeson, Warren (1958)
Harper, Floyd (1927–28–30–31)
Harrell, Cecil (1926)
Harris, Corey (2000–01)
Harris, Dale (1953–54–55–56)
Harris, Jim (1952–53–54–57)
Harvey, George (1923–24)
Haynes, Rodney (1987–88–89–90)
Headdy, Paul* (1929)
Heady, Bob (1963–64)
Heaton, Marvin (1945–47–48–49–50)
Heeter, Bob (1947)
Heifner, Edwin (1922–23–24)
Heifner, Ralph (1924–25–26)
Heinbaugh, Larry (1973–74–75–76)
Heller, Waldemar (1948–49)
Henderson, Jeremy (2003)
Henderson, Mike (1959–60)
Henderson, Craig* (1990)
Henry, David (1921–22)
Henschen, Keith (1964–65)
Hesher, Robert (1933–36)
Hesse, Elmer* (1972)
Hicks, Doug* (1989)
Hill, Todd* (1991–92–93–94–95)
Hodson, Andy* (1997–98–99)
Hole, Merrill (1938–39–40)
Holland, Mike (1969–70)
Hollinger, Scott* (1980–81–82)
Holmes, Basil (1935)
Holmes, Rodney (1991–93)
Holstein, Jim (1974–75–76–77)
Holt, Charles* (1949)
Horn, Dave (1959–60)
Hosier, Mickey (1997–98–99–00)
Howe, Dan (1965)
Howell, Leander (1919)
Howland, Tom (2003)
Huston, Todd* (1991)
Hutcheson, James (1933)
Huth, Dave (1965–66–67)
Icerman, Charles (1933)
Irvin, Dwayne (1977–78–79–80)
Irwin, Rich* (1979–80)
Jackson, Patrick (1999–00–01–02)
Jagla, Ben (1954)
Jahns, Mark (1980–82–83–84)
James, John (1983–84)
James, Markee (1993–94)
Jeffers, John (1942–43)
Jenks, Ron (1959)
Johns, Gerald (1926)
Johns, Jim (1962)
Johnson, Marcus (1991)
Johnson, Norman (1938)
Johnson, Wayne (1996–97–98–99)
Jones, Larry (1982–83–84–85)
Jones, Lem (1987)
Jones, Lonnie (1999–00–01–02)
Jones, Norm (1958–59)
Jones, Todd (1991)
Joris, Matthew (1927–28)
Joyce, Clifford (1942)
Kaiser, Paul (1976–77–79)
Kamiak, Rob (1986–87)
Kaufman, Kim (1974–75)
Kednay, Ed (1972)
Keever, Wayman (1946)
Kehoe, Fred (1949–50)
Keller, Charles (1945)
Kennedy, Barry (1967–68–69)
Kennedy, Robert (1948–49)
Kidd, Curtis (1989–90)
King, Herschell (1932–33)
King, Mark (1984–85)
Kirsch, Brenden * (1997–00)
Kitchel, John (1930–31)
Kitchens, Sam (1967–68)
Koehl, Larry (1957)
Koontz, Robert (1943–46)
Koven, Craig* (1996s)
Kuhny, Bob (1954–55)
Kunze, John (1961–62–63)
Kuzma, Pete (1975–76–77)
Lacey, Marcus (1982–83–84)
Lackey, Ray (1936–37–38)
LaFave, Mike (1984)
Lanich, Gerald (1965–66)
Latham, Ron (1962–63–64)
Law, Roger (1970–71)
Lebo, John (1957–58–59)
Lee, John (1962–63–64)
Lee, John* (1987)
Lee, Scott* (1985)
Lehman, Gene (1951)
Lewellen, John (1935)
Lillie, Gene (1947)
Locke, David* (1948–49–50)
Locke, Howard (1939–40)
Loveless, Raymond (1932)
Lowe, Jack (1956–57)
Loy, Mike* (1993–94)
Luedke, Jon (1985–86)
Lynch, Billy (1998–99–01–02)
Main, Dyson (1921)
Mansbury, Jon (1982–83)
Marshall, Rawle (2001)
Martin, Robert (1996–97)
Mason, Marcus (1996–97–98–99)
Mathias, John (1952)
Matthews, Jamie (1992–93)
McCallum, Ray (1980–81–82–83)
McCammon, Harold (1929–30–31–32)
McCarter, Phil (1949–50–51)
McCarty, Gerald (1941–42)
McClain, Bill (1948–49–50)
McCollom, Matt (2002–03)
McColly, Bill (1949–50–51)
McComas, Charles (1922)
McCune, Bob (1961)
McCurdy, Paris (1989–90)
McKenzie, Robert (1946–47)
Mendenhall, John (1942–43)
Mercer, Mark (1933–35)
Merica, Larry* (1965–66)
Meyer, Bill* (1977–78)
Meyer, Paul (1935–36–37)
Meyer, Ron* (1976–77–78)
Middleton, Nick* (2000–01)
Miggenburg, Marty (1970–71–72)
Miller, Carl (1957–61)
Miller, Gary (1968–69)
Miller, Greg (1987–88–89–90)
Miller, John (1966–67–68)
Miller, Ken* (1957–58)
Miller, Stew (1966–67–68)
Minglin, Aaron* (2002–03)
Minnick, George (1946)
Moniaci, Steve* (1976–77–78–79)
Moodie, Cedric (1999–00–01)
Moore, Marzine (1968–69–70)
Morgan, Jess (1926)
Morgan, Warner* (1947)
Mossburg, Oscar (1922)
Moudy, Larry (1962–63)
Mount, Verner* (1930)
Muller, Roman (1989–90)
Mullet, Ron* (1976–77–78)
Murray, Josh (1999–00–01)
Murrell, Clement (1978–79–80–81)
Nay William* (1951–52)
Neal, Stan (1963–64–65)
Neese, Lowell (1920)
Neff, Ken (1951)
Newton, Bob (1950–51–52)
Nichols, Scott (1987–88–89–90)
Nixon, Bill (1960)
Norris, Marcus (1995–96)
Oaks, Mike (1972)
Oldham, Dick (1961–62)

O'Neal, Bill (1959–60–61)
Oren, Don (1932)
Owens, Robert (2001–02–03)
Page. Walter (1947)
Palombizio, Dan (1985–86)
Parker, Jeff (1979–80–81–82)
Parks, Roger (1960)
Parrish, Larry (1974)
Parrish, Shawn (1989–90)
Patterson, Steve*(1984–85–86–87–88)
Payne, Steve (1993–94–95)
Pensinger, Leslie (1919)
Perry, Larry (1958)
Peters, Ron (1984–85)
Peterson, Billy (1943)
Pettijohn, Harold (1924)
Phenis, Greg (1970)
Poteet, Jim (1954–55)
Powell, Fred (1951–52–53)
Price, James (1925)
Pursley, Robert (1945)
Ray, Tim (1996–97)
Readnour, Mike (1960–61–62)
Reed, Floyd (1948–49–50)
Reed, Larry (1985–86)
Reed, Ryan (1995–96–97–98)
Reeder, Chris (1971–72)
Reedy, Dick (1963–64)
Reedy, Larry (1965)
Regenold, Jim (1970–71–72)
Reid, Doug (1965–66)
Reid, Robert (1940–41–42)
Renner, Everett (1927–28–30)
Resler, Herb*(1962–63)
Ricks, Steve (1966–68–69)
Rigdon, Ralph (1921)
Riemenschneider, Bill (1946)
Rightsell, Glendon (1921)
Riley, Fred (1945–46–47)
Rinehart, Herb (1954)
Risinger, Ed (1939–40)
Risinger, Joe (1936–37–38)
Risinger, Robert (1938–39–40)
Robbins, Jeff (1991–92)
Robbins, Rob (2000–01–02)
Rogers, DeWayne (1995)
Roland, Lamont (1998)
Ross, Milt (1953)
Rowley, Bill* (1974)
Rowray, Rick (1984–85–86)
Rudicel, Max (1936–37)
Rudicel, Rex (1936–37–38)
Sample, Ernest (1940–41)
Sapp, Mike (1965–66)
Satterfield, Ray (1963)
Sawyer, Mack (1966–67)
Schings, Chris* (1977)
Schmeltz, Jack (1954–55–56)
Schneider, David (1951)
Schooler, Virgil (1925–28)
Schurr, Terry (1956–57–58)
Scott, Allan (1979–80–81–82)
Scott, David (1982–83)
Scudder, Ralph (1919)
Selwa, Dan (1968–69)
Sering, Harold (1935–37)
Sexton, Jack (1948–49–50)
Shanks, Oris (1920–21–23–24)
Shaw, Orrin (1924–25)
Shelton, Chris (1983–84–85–86)
Shively, Everett (1927–28–29–30)
Shook, Forrest (1936–37–38)
Showalter, Keith (1937)
Shuck, Ned (1935–36)
Shumaker, Mike (1966–67)
Shumm, Al (1925–26)
Simons, Mike* (1966–67)
Simpson, Wayne (1942)
Sims, Robert (1977–78)
Slick, Brian (1988)
Slick, Paul (1952–53)
Small, Jeff* (1985–86)
Smilock, Harold* (1930)
Smith, Charles (1986–87)
Smith, Charles (1995–96–97–98)
Smith, Clayton (1941–42)
Smith, George (1927–28–29)
Smith, Richard (1970)
Smith, Steve (1995–96)
Smith, Theron (2000–01–02)
Smuts, Jacob* (1933)
Snapp, Jim* (1982–83–84)
Snider, Nelson (1920–21–22)
Spence, Quention (1974–75)
Spencer, Aaron* (1988)
Spicer, Mike (1989–90–91–92)
Stacy, Bob* (1992–93–94–95)
Stalling, Keith (1989–91–92)
Starkey, Norm* (1959–60)
Stealy, Dick (1939–40–41)
Stebbins, John* (1933)
Stewart, Bob (1959–60–61)
Stewart, George (1951)
Stillabower, Terry (1967–68)
Stoops, Elden (1943)
Stout, Howard (1940–41–42)
Stout, Marvin (1936–37–38)
Straight, Bob (1947–48–49–50)
Strohm, Carl* (1948)
Stultz, David* (1997)
Sturgeon, Tim* (1987–88)
Suggs, Shafer (1973–74–75)
Sullivan, Jim (1958–59)
Swinford, Basil (1921)
Sylvester, Jeermal (1991–92–93–94)
Taylor, George (1958, 1959, 1960)
Thompson, Chandler (1990–91–92)
Thompson, LaSalle (1995–96)
Thompson, Terry (1953)
Thurston, Dan (1961–62–63)
Thurston, Mark (1979–80–81)
Till, Rick* (1993–94)
Tincher, Don* (1982–83–84–85)
Todd, Paul (1933)
Toler, Charles (1927–28–29–30)
Trees, Phillip* (1945)
Tribbett, Paul* (1956)
Troutwine, Jim (1971–72–73)
Truex, Greg (1966)
Truman, Tom* (1971–72–73)
Tucker, Steve (1970)
Tummers, Tim* (1987–88–89–90)
Turner, Keith* (1992–93)
Turner, Steve (1991–92–93)
Ulm, Christopher* (2001–02–03)
Underhill, Phil (1966–67–68)
VanSickle, Wayne (1955–56–57)
Wagoner, Jason (1991)
Walker, John (1927–28)
Wallace, Tom (1951)
Walradth, Bob (1943)
Wantz, Michael*(1994–95–96–97)
Ware, Noel (1920)
Wehr, Wayne (1961)
Welch, Chris* (1988–89)
Wells, Bonzi (1995–96–97–98)
Welmer, Dave (1976–77–78–79)
Wesley, Derrick (1985–86–87–88)
West, Brian* (1984–85–86)
White, Mike (1975–76)
Whitehead, Reggie (1994)
Whittington, John (1984–86)
Whitworth, Dick* (1952–53–54)
Wilkison, Howard (1961–62)
Williams Chris (2002)
Williams, Jeff (1978–79–80–81)
Williams, John (1980–81–82)
Williams, R.J. (1997)
Willingham, Zach (2002)
Willis, Byron* (1935)
Wilmore, John (1927–28)
Wilson, Mel (1933–35)
Winders, Matt (1992–93–94)
Womack, Maurice (1982–83)
Yestingsmeier, Earl* (1954–55)
Young, Walter (1930)
Zachary, Randy (1994–95–96–97)
Zello, Ed (1988)
Zickgraff, Andy* (1997–98)
Ziesig, Jason* (2002–03)

* Denotes Student Manager

Appendix B

Ball State Men's Basketball Most Valuable Players—A.L. (Pete) Phillips Award

Mike Readnour	1960–61
Ed Butler	1961–62
Ed Butler	1962–63
Ed Butler	1963–64
Stan Neal	1964–65
Mack Sawyer	1965–66
Mack Sawyer	1966–67
John Miller	1967–68
Gary Miller & Mike Holland	1968–69
Mike Holland	1969–70
Jim Regenold	1970–71
Jim Regenold	1971–72
Larry Bullington	1972–73
Larry Bullington	1973–74
Bob Faulkner and Kim Kaufman	1974–75
Randy Boarden	1975–76
Jim Hahn	1976–77
Robert Sims	1977–78
Randy Boarden	1978–79
Ray McCallum	1979–80
Ray McCallum	1980–81
C.C. Fullove	1981–82
Ray McCallum	1982–83
Jeff Furlin and Marcus Lacey	1983–84
Dan Palombizio	1984–85
Dan Palombizio	1985–86
Charles Smith and Derrick Wesley	1986–87
Derrick Wesley	1987–88
Curtis Kidd	1988–89
Paris McCurdy	1989–90
Chandler Thompson	1990–91
Keith Stalling	1991–92
Jamie Matthews	1992–93
Steve Payne	1993–94
Steve Payne	1994–95
Bonzi Wells	1995–96
Bonzi Wells	1996–97
Bonzi Wells	1997–98
Marcus Mason	1998–99
Duane Clemens	1999–00
Patrick Jackson	2000–01
Patrick Jackson and Theron Smith	2001–02
Chris Williams	2002–03

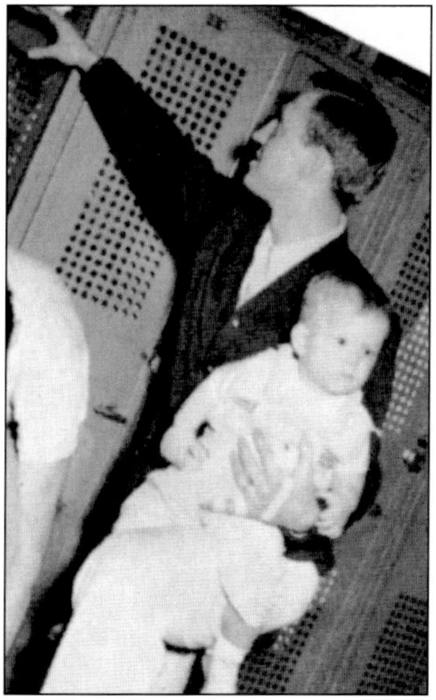

The way it once was, as a player from the 1948-49 team dresses in the locker room, combining basketball with babysitting.